Getting into

Business & Economics Course

Getting into guides

Getting into

Business & Economics Courses

Carly Roberts

10th edition

trotman | **t**

For Mandy and Kelvin

Getting into Business & Economics Courses

This 10th edition published in 2013 by Trotman Publishing, an imprint of Crimson Publishing Limited, Westminster House, Kew Road, Richmond, Surrey TW9 2ND

© Trotman Publishing 2013

Author: Carly Roberts
9th edn by James Burnett published in 2011 as *Getting Into Business & Economics Courses*
8th edn by James Burnett published in 2009 as *Getting Into Business, Economics & Management Courses*
6th and 7th edns by Kate Smith published in 2005 and 2007 as *Getting Into Business & Management Courses*
3rd, 4th and 5th edns by Fiona Hindle published in 1999, 2001 and 2003 as *Getting Into Business, Economics & Management Courses*
1st and 2nd edns published in 1994 and 1996 as *Getting Into Accountancy, Business Studies and Economics*

Editions 1–7 published by Trotman and Co. Ltd

British Library Cataloguing in Publication Data
A catalogue record for this book is available from the British Library

ISBN 978 1 90604 190 8

Tables of UCAS tariff point systems under 'Further information' (Chapter 11) reprinted with permission from UCAS.

Typeset by IDSUK (DataConnection) Ltd
Printed and bound in the UK by Ashford Colour Press, Gosport, Hants

Contents

Contents

About the author

Carly Roberts is a Director of Studies and Careers and University Adviser at Mander Portman Woodward. Carly has previously worked for UCAS and a number of universities and colleges, advising students on all aspects of the admissions process.

Acknowledgements

I would like to thank James Burnett, Kate Smith and Fiona Hindle who wrote the previous versions of this book, *Getting Into Business, Economics & Management Courses*. Thanks should also go to Steve Cook, an education consultant, for his contributions to the economics sections, and to Sarah Ratcliffe, Nina Nguyen, Dolly Duan and the many other people who helped with this and earlier editions. Special thanks also go to those who shared their experiences in the case studies sections, and to the numerous university admissions tutors who gave an insight into what they are looking for. On a personal note, I would like to thank my family for their support and encouragement.

As far as I am aware, all information in this book is correct at the time of going to press. Unless stated otherwise, the views expressed in this book are my own.

I hope you find this guide useful and wish you every success for the future.

Carly Roberts

For up-to-date information on business, economics and related financial and management courses, please visit www.mpw.co.uk.

Introduction

The title of this book should really be *Getting into Business, Economics, Management, Accounting, Finance, Banking and Related Courses*, because it covers all of these subjects – and more. But then there would not have been enough room on the cover for my name, so we decided on the shortened version instead. First and foremost, this guide aims to provide information and strategies for students interested in applying to study any of the subjects listed above. The details and advice in the book are relevant to applications for courses such as accounting and finance, banking and econometrics, and for joint honours courses such as mathematics and economics.

Following a career in business, economics, management or a related area is a very popular option for graduates, and students choose courses in this sector for a variety of reasons. They gain the opportunity to develop their knowledge of management and domestic and international business by studying a range of theories, companies and organisations and by learning about and gaining practical experience of tasks such as business plans, negotiation and giving presentations. The courses are wide-ranging and help students develop a number of different professional, administrative, communication and technical skills to prepare them successfully for a future job in the field. Graduates with degrees in business, economics, management and so on can go on to such diverse careers as advertising, banking and finance, insurance and teaching.

About this book

This book is designed to give you an overview of the whole application process.

Chapter 1 looks at the types of business and economics courses available. Chapter 2 covers work experience and the importance of internships in strengthening your application.

Chapter 3 gives advice on how to choose universities and courses and what to consider – both academically and non-academically. In Chapter 4, we look at the UCAS application and suggested timescale for completing your application. Chapter 5 then covers the all-important personal statement and how to maximise your chances of your application being successful.

In Chapter 6 you'll find out how to have a successful university interview – in terms of both preparation and how to behave in the interview itself. We also look at current economics issues and business case studies that may be useful during your interview preparation.

Chapter 7 is for anyone who is not putting forward a standard application to university; mature students as well as international students can find useful information here.

Once you have made your application, you'll need to know what happens next. Chapter 8 looks at all of your options once you receive your results, whether they were what you wanted or not.

Chapter 9 covers fees and the types of funding you may be eligible for.

Chapter 10 discusses some of the career areas that you might think about applying to once you have graduated. This chapter goes into detail about making the first steps in your career and the options open to business and economics graduates.

Finally, Chapter 11 looks at where you can find further information and also gives the UCAS tariff points tables for courses in business and economics. At the back of the book you will find a glossary of terms relating to business, economics and university admission.

This book is not meant to be a reference manual in which you look up a particular point in the contents page and go to that section: rather, it is meant to be read from the beginning to give you a complete overview of the subject, preferably well in advance of your application.

Throughout the book, the examples that quote university entrance requirements use A level and AS level grades. However, the advice is applicable to students studying Scottish Highers, the International Baccalaureate, Pre-University (Pre-U) and other qualifications. The UCAS website (www.ucas.com) lists entrance requirements for all of the major examination systems in its 'Course Search' section. If you are unsure about what you need to achieve, individual universities will be happy to give you advice; contact details are given on all of their websites.

In essence, if you are considering working in this field, this guide is designed to help you explore the entry routes and options in higher education to start you on your career.

What do businesses do?

In its widest sense, a business is an organisation that exists to fulfil the purpose decided by its owners. This definition shows us just how varied and different businesses can be. Usually, a business has to make a surplus on its trading (a profit) to be able to continue into the following year, but not all business owners see the profit motive as the single most important factor. Firms in leisure and tourism, the music industry or the media are all examples of businesses that are driven by the passions of those involved. Yes, some are also highly successful financially, but it would be wrong to say that money was the sole driving force.

Even those firms that might be regarded as more mainstream are increasingly aware of the image that they present to the general public and feel that this has to be taken into consideration alongside profits.

Businesses also vary greatly in their size: some are small, family-run concerns, others are vast public corporations. Many multinationals are much larger than some countries. Of the top 100 entities in the world in terms of annual turnover, about half are multinationals and the other half are countries. Working for such large organisations will obviously feel completely different from working for small- to medium-sized enterprises (SMEs) employing fewer than 250 people.

Whatever the size of the business, there are many differing approaches to running it in the best way. Business managers fulfil a variety of tasks and need a whole range of different skills. They need to inspire and give leadership, research, analyse and present information, think laterally to come up with imaginative answers, communicate with many different types of people, organise their own time and work to tight deadlines, design complex business strategies, solve conundrums, and trade one interest off against another. Jobs in business are never dull because the business world is constantly changing; firms are always up against their competitors on the one hand and changing consumer habits on the other. Even very big firms are not immune to failure and decline. The recent problems that have affected Toyota (see Chapter 6) are a good illustration of this.

The way a business is run in practice is referred to as the corporate culture. This includes all of those many things that give the company its character. There are a number of different philosophies on best business practice and a variety of so-called business gurus write books and run seminars about their ideas. Tom Peters, Peter Drucker and Charles Handy are some of the more famous gurus, but there are also more obscure approaches such as *Our Iceberg is Melting: Changing and Succeeding Under Any Conditions* or *Winnie-the-Pooh on Management*. Cartoons such as Dilbert point out just how often managers get it wrong and how frustrating this is for their subordinates.

What do economists do?

Economics is the study of how individuals and groups make choices in a world where their needs and desires outweigh the availability of resources. Economics is a social science relating to every aspect of our lives, from the choices we make as individuals to the decisions made by governments across the globe.

Economics graduates may find jobs in banking, insurance or tax, as well as with governments and large organisations such as the Bank of England. Some become academic or professional economists who develop economic theories; others manage money for either investment banks or governments. Some economics graduates follow careers in accountancy or management. Others work in the transport, manufacturing, communications, insurance or retail industries. Employers value students who have studied economics because they have well-developed analytical and critical thinking skills and are good at problem solving. Economists learn to make decisions and come to conclusions based on the analysis of numerical evidence: what are called economic indicators. Economic indicators include things such as unemployment figures, exchange rates, share prices, inflation rates and gross domestic product (GDP).

Economists use these indicators to assess whether markets or economies are likely to improve or worsen, and then to act accordingly. This could be on a small scale – deciding whether it is sensible for a company to invest in building a new factory in another country – or on a much larger scale – should a government raise or lower interest rates to try to influence the inflation rate.

Economics can be split into two broad areas: microeconomics and macroeconomics. Microeconomics looks at the behaviour of markets and consumers, including how businesses price their goods and consumer spending habits (such as why they buy a more expensive brand of washing-up liquid when a cheaper one is available). It also looks at the small-scale decisions that affect our daily lives. If petrol prices rise, should you get rid of your car? Are higher wages an incentive to work harder or to work for fewer hours? It analyses different markets, from monopolies and oligopolies to situations where there is proper competition between suppliers. Macroeconomics, on the other hand, is the study of economies as a whole, and looks at issues that have an impact on a country's financial situation; for example, inflation, balance of payments, exchange rates and the relationships between these. Macroeconomic issues are often the main headlines on the news or in your paper – particularly at the moment!

What do accountants do?

There are many different types of accountant, but one thing they have in common is that they analyse financial data and present it in a form that allows interested parties to understand what is happening in a company or business. Management accountants, for example, analyse budgets, sales and costs to allow the bosses to assess the past, present or future success of the business. Another type of accountant is the auditor, whose role is to check that money is not being wasted or mismanaged. For a more complete picture, look at the Chartered Institute of Management Accountants' website (www.cimaglobal.com).

What do managers do?

Well, they manage things – people, organisations, communication paths, the goods or services that a business sells, and many other things besides. More about different management roles and responsibilities can be found on the Chartered Management Institute's website (www.managers.org.uk). Management is essentially the art of making things happen through people. The word 'manager' is used in almost every walk of life, from sport to banks, from shops to IT. Managers are also referred to as supervisors, project leaders, heads of department . . . the list is almost endless. Managers utilise a range of skills, but primarily they need the ability to organise people and processes, to communicate or motivate effectively, and to relay the company's aims to the people underneath them in its hierarchy.

Once you have thought about possible areas of study or your future career options, your next stage is to do some first-hand research. This means talking to people who have experience of studying and working in these fields. A good starting point is looking at university websites, as these will often include case histories of current students and graduates. Some universities offer a 'contact a student' option, so you can discuss what it is like to study one of these courses with a current student. You should also talk to careers advisers and people who are working in businesses or as economists or accountants.

Competition for places

The competition for places at the higher-ranking universities is intense, and many candidates, while successfully gaining a place on an economics or business-related degree course, do so either through Clearing or at one of their lower-preference universities. Employers hold different courses and institutions at different levels of esteem, and so you should do all that you can to ensure that your choice of university will stand you in good stead in the future.

There is particular competition for places on economics and management courses, with more applicants than places available. For example, UCAS reports that there were around 15,500 applications and about

7,300 students accepted onto economics courses for 2012 entry. At the top-ranked universities, there can be as many as 15 to 20 applicants for every place. On average UK students were more successful in getting these places than overseas students, with a 75% success rate in 2012 (according to UCAS), compared to 54% of EU students and 52% for international students. This could be due to better knowledge of the UCAS system and access to well informed advisors.

The golfer Gary Player is said to have responded to accusations of being a 'lucky' golfer by saying 'the harder I work, the luckier I get'. Bear this in mind when considering your application to university. While there is a small element of luck involved in getting offers from universities, success is mainly down to planning (and, of course, working hard to achieve the best grades you can). You need to make sure you research your courses properly. Look at the websites of the universities you are considering and check if you are likely to meet the entry criteria. You can even contact them to ask for advice on how to strengthen your application through activities such as work experience. Because of the competition for places on highly ranked courses, it is particularly important to ensure that the personal statement section of your UCAS application is constructed carefully, and that your predicted grades are high enough for your first-choice universities to consider you.

1 | Studying business, economics and related courses

In 2012, UCAS listed 3,543 business courses, 1,166 economics programmes and 868 finance-related courses in the UK. So how do you decide which course is for you? This chapter looks at narrowing these courses down to the maximum of five that will end up on your UCAS application. It's a daunting prospect so we'll be looking at what questions you should be asking before you make that important final selection.

Different courses available

What's in a name?

You are considering a career in a business- or finance-related field, and you want to find a suitable university course that will help you achieve this. The university prospectuses that you sent off for have arrived, so you settle down in a comfortable chair to read through them and begin to make your choice of course. Two hours later, you are bewildered: should you choose business studies, business and management studies, management science or business management? What is the difference between banking and finance, and international banking? Would a potential employer favour economics over econometrics? Why do some universities offer mathematics with economics whereas others teach only mathematics and economics? Well, after reading this chapter you should have a clearer idea about the course you should consider.

Let us look at the courses listed on the website of that prestigious (but fictional!) institution, Barton University:

- accounting and finance
- banking and finance
- business and management studies
- business mathematics and statistics
- business studies
- econometrics and mathematical economics
- economics
- financial economics
- management (three-year course)

- management (four-year sandwich course)
- management sciences
- mathematics and economics.

The first thing to be aware of is that there is considerable overlap between many of these courses. For example, as part of the business studies degree course, you would attend lectures on management – the same lectures that the management students attend. Additionally, in the second and third years of the course you will be offered options for the courses you wish to study, so you would be able to steer your degree towards the areas that interested you most. This brings us to the three important rules when it comes to choosing your courses:

- **Rule Number 1.** Read through the course content for all three or four years of the course. Do not choose a course just because of its title. You will find that the content of a particular course varies from university to university, and that there is considerable choice available within a particular university's course. This is important to know if you are interviewed (see Chapter 6), as you may well be asked to explain why you have chosen that course. Being able to discuss the course structure in detail will be an important factor in convincing the interviewer that you are a serious applicant.

Similar-sounding courses often have very different entrance requirements in terms of both preferred A level subjects and grade requirements. A degree in econometrics is likely to require a higher level of mathematical ability (possibly further mathematics to AS level or even A level) than economics, and some universities will differentiate between their 'preferred' A level subjects (the more traditional A levels such as mathematics, history, physics or economics) and 'non-preferred' subjects (general studies, art and media studies are examples of subjects that some universities do not favour). Again, careful reading of the prospectus is important, because each university will have its own preferences or requirements.

The entrance requirements for degree courses will always specify what examination results are necessary. These are expressed either as grade requirements (for example, AAB) or tariff points (for example, 300 – see Chapter 11). When you apply through UCAS (unless you are applying post-results; that is, during your gap year), your teachers will put your predicted grades in your reference. You need to find out in advance what they are going to predict, because this will affect your choice of universities and courses. There is no point in applying for five university courses that require ABB if your A level predictions are CCC; you will be rejected by all of your choices and you will then need to try to find alternatives through the UCAS Extra scheme, or through Clearing (see Chapter 8). Similarly, if you are predicted to achieve AAA, you are probably aiming too low if all of the courses you are applying for require DDD at A level. As a rough guide, if you are predicted, say, ABB, you might want to choose three courses that require ABB, one that requires BBB and a course that demands BBC. This means that you have a good chance of getting a number of offers but it also gives you options if you do not quite meet the grade requirements when you get your results (see Chapter 8). If you want to apply for a course that requires grades higher than those you have been predicted, it might be worth contacting the admissions department at that university to ask for advice before completing your UCAS application. If you exceed your predicted grades you may be eligible for Adjustment (see Chapter 8). So, rules 2 and 3 are as follows.

- **Rule Number 2.** Research the entrance requirements for each course and for each university, and narrow down your options by finding the courses whose requirements most closely match your A level subjects and likely grades.
- **Rule Number 3.** Find out what your grade predictions are and base your course choices on these.

We will now look at some of the Barton University courses in more detail. Bear in mind that courses with similar titles can differ significantly from university to university. These snapshots should be taken as an indication of what the courses involve but should not form the entirety of your research. Your choices should be based on a thorough investigation of each university's course details, either in the prospectus or on the website.

Accounting and finance

Accounting and finance courses look at the financial aspects of companies and businesses. You will study accounting techniques, how companies assess their financial performance and how they plan for the future. They also cover aspects of management, share dealing and the way companies are perceived by the public and by potential investors.

Courses you will take as part of the degree could include:

- elements of accounting and finance
- introduction to statistics
- managerial accounting
- principles of finance
- economic theories
- management science
- business mathematics
- commercial law.

Economics and econometrics

Economics is the study of income and expenditure, from small-scale situations (households or businesses) to global issues (how countries deal with income, spending, inflation and employment). It covers topics such as setting the price of goods, inflation, balance of payments and unemployment. Econometrics looks at how statistical methods are used to analyse and test economic theories.

Courses you will take as part of the degree could include:

- microeconomics
- macroeconomics
- mathematical methods
- statistics
- econometrics
- development economics
- accounting and finance
- game theory
- international economics
- labour economics.

Management

Management courses look at how organisations work effectively. The course will cover a broad range of topics, such as the structure of an organisation, financial management and how people can be managed to get the best out of them. Management science is the study of how management methods are underpinned by analytical techniques and mathematical models.

Courses that you will take as part of your degree could include:

- economics
- psychology and behavioural science
- accounting and finance
- the process of management
- economics for management
- management science
- law.

Business studies

Business studies courses look at how businesses are run. A successful business model comprises a whole range of different aspects, from marketing, advertising, location and markets, through to financial issues and management. It is a practical rather than theoretical subject, focusing on problem solving and real-life situations.

Courses that you will take as part of your degree could include:

- accounting
- organisational behaviour
- economics
- management science

- a market or business project
- international business
- marketing.

As you can see, there is a great deal of crossover in the topics covered by these courses. A management degree will include some accounting, economics and business courses, and an economics degree will include aspects of accounting, management, finance and business. Business studies courses include modules on accounting, management and economics. Figure 1 will give you an indication of the links between these courses, and the differences between them.

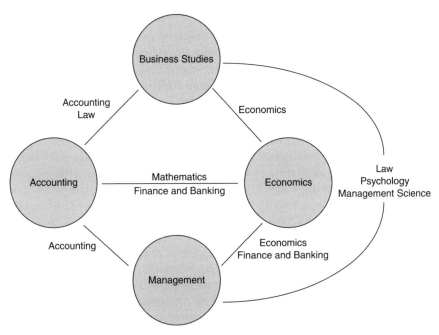

Figure 1 Degree courses showing common links between disciplines

Case study

'I didn't study maths or economics at A level and this made the first term a little harder for me than for other students on the course, but I quickly caught up. The thing that surprised me most was that economics requires a different approach from other subjects, because you have to think in a more abstract way, and adapt and apply the economic models you are taught to real-life situations. There are formulaic ways to solve these problems – you have to approach them from many different angles, and to learn to try to comprehend the situations before trying to answer questions.'

Steve, former economics student, London School of Economics

Single or joint honours?

If you are considering a single honours course, bear in mind that a good range of optional subjects might make it even more inviting. You might not want to be stuck with just a handful of choices from which to fill in your timetable after you have put down the core courses. Options may come from a similar field or a completely different discipline. Pinpointing specific subjects that you would like to study in your degree can help narrow your choice of university.

Most business and management courses include the core subjects of finance, economics, law, marketing, management and human resources.

In addition, most offer a range of options in the major areas of business such as marketing, finance, human resources, supply chain manage-ment, international business and trade, business strategy and small business management. Taking some relevant options may make you more attractive to a particular employer.

Alternatively, if you want to specialise in one other area, a joint honours degree might be more appealing. Some joint degrees do not require previous knowledge of the second subject. Others, especially those with a European language or a science-based discipline, often specify that candidates must have an A level, AS level or GCSE qualification, or equivalent, in a specific subject. In joint degrees, be wary of courses that have similar titles, such as 'Business with German' and 'Business and German'. In the former, business is the major subject and German is the minor, but in the second, which is more likely to involve a year abroad, you will probably spend equal time on each subject. Economics and mathematical subjects go well together because economics is a theoretical subject, underpinned by mathematics and statistical meth-ods. You will find a wide range of courses that combine economics with mathematics and/or statistics. For strong mathematicians, some of these courses may be easier to get offers for than the single honours economics courses. However, do not think that this is an easy way to get to study economics at a top university. These degrees will involve the study of mathematical topics to a high level, and so you need to be interested in mathematical subjects (and good at them) to get onto this type of course.

Exemptions

Are you thinking about going into accountancy, banking or insurance? Most commerce-related degrees contain modules that will give you exemptions from some of the examinations that aspiring professionals are obliged to sit for organisations such as the Chartered Institute of Marketing, the Chartered Institute of Personnel and Development and the various accountancy bodies. If you are concerned about which exemption subjects you can include in your degree, call the universities and ask which of the professional bodies recognise their courses.

Alternatively, you can get in touch with individual professional bodies directly and they will tell you which university courses are officially accredited. Although taking exemptions as part of a degree course can be convenient, it is not disastrous for your career if you do not – but your professional qualifications may take around an extra six months to complete.

Placements and overseas study

Studying abroad and/or completing a work placement could also be factors that affect your degree selection. It is possible to study business and management in dozens of countries across the globe as part of a degree based at a British university. Not all of these courses send you off for a full year, though: there are schemes that last for only one term or a semester. You do not need to be a linguist either, because it is always possible to study overseas in an English-speaking location such as North America, South Africa, Australia or Malaysia. The availability of student exchanges has increased through programmes such as Erasmus, which encourage universities to provide international opportunities where practical – particularly in Europe. And the popularity of overseas study has encouraged some universities to develop special exchange relationships with universities further afield.

Methods of assessment and study

Degrees are usually assessed through a combination of examinations (normally spread over two or three years) and coursework, although individual units may be assessed purely by coursework or dissertation. Methods of studying, such as lectures, seminars, tutorials, practicals, workshops and self-study, tend not to vary much between universities (except for Oxford and Cambridge, where they centre on the one-to-one tutorial system). Some institutions, however, do offer part-time courses and even distance learning for a few of their degrees.

2| Getting work experience

It is no secret that university admissions tutors like work experience. Being able to demonstrate your commitment to and knowledge of your chosen area could mean the difference between being offered a place on a course or not. What's more, a recent study of the graduate market in 2012 by High Fliers Research found that more than half of the top 100 UK graduate recruiters say those with no previous work experience are unlikely to be selected for a job after university. This section will look at using work experience to make your UCAS application stand out and the importance of getting internships and work placements while at university.

Work experience

Getting some relevant work experience has become more valuable in recent years, and is considered essential by some university admissions tutors. In a climate where getting into business, economics or management is so fiercely competitive, it is not enough just to be a brilliant academic. One of the things that an admissions tutor will look for is how serious you are about your chosen course. Many students decide to apply for a business- or finance-related course at university because they think it will be an easy route to becoming rich rather than because they are actually interested in the course content and the skills that they will acquire from their studies. Work experience or work-shadowing is an ideal way to demonstrate your commitment and show that you have done some research. If you can write about things that you saw or did on your work placement, and how they related to your A level studies, proposed university course or future career, you will be a much more attractive proposition to the university selectors.

If you have decided to take a gap year, it is a good idea to spend at least part of it getting some experience relevant to your degree. This will be valuable during your course and will appeal to employers once you have graduated.

In addition, the more (ideally relevant) experience you have, the better your chance of succeeding in your initial job applications. Many employers will rate work experience as being almost as important as academic qualifications.

What will you gain from work experience?

- It will add weight to your personal statement.
- It will give you a true insight into the business or financial world and whether or not it is what you want to do. Some real experience will be particularly useful if you are trying to weigh up which area of business you'd like to go into. For example, are you more analytical or creative? Would you be more suited to a career in finance or marketing?
- It helps you to make a better transition from education into the world of full-time work.
- It gives you the opportunity to build up those all-important contacts.
- It gives you a more impressive curriculum vitae (CV) – and will help you to gain excellent references (with luck!), which are important for any future career.

However, it is not that easy getting relevant work experience. Most admissions tutors and employers recognise this and do not stipulate that it is essential, although it is preferred. If you cannot get experience in a large business, any work experience that demonstrates your use of the skills employers are interested in will be valuable. Communication skills, determination, commercial awareness and IT skills can all be developed in many other sectors of business and commerce.

'What do I look for first in a personal statement? Work experience. Why? Because it shows that the student has thought about their future studies and done some research. It also makes for a much more interesting personal statement because they can write about what they observed and why it is relevant, so I am more likely to offer them a place. What students don't always appreciate is that my main jobs in the university are teaching and research. Being involved in admissions is an extra (albeit very enjoyable) burden. I tend to read the UCAS applications in the evenings after work, and might get through over a hundred in a night, and so the ones that make me interested in the applicant are more likely to go on the "offer" pile.'

An admissions tutor for economics

Looking for work experience

Marketing yourself

There is no single guaranteed way of getting work experience, so try as many ways as you can think of, and be creative in the process. Here are a few suggestions.

- Ask your teachers at school/college if they have any contacts in the business world.
- Use your careers library and speak to your careers officer.
- Talk to your family and friends and ask them whether they can suggest anyone to contact.
- Make sure everyone you know is aware you are looking for work experience.
- Send your CV and a covering letter to a variety of local businesses.
- Keep up to date by reading the business pages of the quality press.
- Watch and listen to the business programmes on television and radio.
- Look around at volunteering websites for opportunities relevant to your area of interest.

If you have a contact in a local organisation, try asking to go in for one or two weeks' work experience during the holidays, or even ask for one day's work-shadowing to get an insight into what the business environment is like. Whichever route you take, it will almost certainly be on a voluntary basis unless you have specific skills to offer, such as good office and keyboard skills. If that is the case, you could try to get some paid work during the summer or register with an employment agency.

How to put together a CV to apply for work experience

It is never too early to start to put together a CV. This is a summary of what you have done in your life to date. If you have hardly any work experience, then one page on good-quality A4 paper will be sufficient. If you are a mature student with a lot of jobs behind you, there is sometimes a case for going onto a second page, but for most young people a brief CV will be appropriate. The main headings to cover are described below.

Name; contact details; date of birth; nationality

These are the basic details to head your CV. Make sure they're right!

Education and qualifications

Start with your present course of study and work back to the beginning of secondary school. No primary schools please! List the qualifications with grades you already have and the ones you intend to sit.

Work experience

Start with the most recent. Don't worry if you have had only a Saturday job at the local shop or a paper round. Put it all down. Employers would rather see that you have done something, and every job will teach you some skills, such as reliability or retail skills.

Skills

List everything you do that could have a commercial application, such as computer skills, software packages used, typing, languages, driving licence and so on.

Interests and positions of responsibility

What do you like to do in your spare time? If you hold or have held any positions of responsibility, such as captain of a sports team, been a committee member or head boy or girl at school, put it all down. Do you play an instrument or have a creative hobby? Do you belong to a society or club? All these say something about the person you are.

Referees

You should usually mention two referees: an academic one, such as a teacher or head of your school, plus someone who knows you well personally but is not a relative, such as someone you have worked for.

Always highlight your good points on a CV and do not leave gaps. Always account for your time. If something such as illness prevented you from reaching your potential in your exams, point this out in your covering letter. To succeed in business you need to have excellent attention to detail, so make sure your spelling and grammar are perfect! Lay out your CV clearly and logically and include any exams you are studying for as well as those you have already taken. The box below offers an example.

A sample CV

Lucy Mathilda Johnson

Address 1 Melchester Road, Melchester MC2 3EF

Telephone 0123 456 7890   **email** lmj@melchester.sch.uk
Date of birth 1 January 1995   **Nationality** British

Education 2006–2013: Melchester High School
2013: A levels to be taken: Geography, German, Mathematics
2012: AS level: Psychology (B)
2011: GCSEs: English (A), Mathematics (A), Geography (A), German (A), Biology (B), Chemistry (B), History (C), Physics (C)

Work experience
2011–2013 (Saturdays)
Sales assistant in busy dry cleaners in centre of York.
August 2012
Two weeks as temporary receptionist in small firm of accountants, responsible for answering telephone and general clerical work.

2009–2011 (Saturdays)
Delivering newspapers and magazines throughout my local area.

Skills
Modern languages: good written and spoken German.
IT: competent in MS Word and Excel, good keyboard skills.

Positions of responsibility
Captain of school netball team, treasurer for Young Enterprise
company.

Interests
Netball, swimming, reading, travel and music.

References
Available on request.

The covering letter

Every CV or application form should always be accompanied by a covering letter. The letter is important because it is usually the first thing a
potential employer reads. Here are some tips on structuring and presenting your letter.

- The letter should be on the same plain A4 paper as your CV and
  should look like a professional business document. Do not use lined
  paper, and keep it to one side only.
- Try to find out the name of the person to whom you should send your
  letter and CV. It makes a great difference to the reader if you can
  personalise your application – but do not be overly familiar. Use their
  title (Mr, Ms, Dr, etc.) and last name, not 'Dear Bob'. (Get a book on
  business letter writing if you need help with the conventions. For
  example, if you start the letter 'Dear Mr Brown' remember you
  should finish it 'Yours sincerely'. If you do not know the recipient's
  name and send it, for example, to the personnel manager, begin with
  'Dear Sir or Madam' and finish with 'Yours faithfully'.)
- The first paragraph should tell the reader why you are contacting
  them (e.g. 'I am writing to enquire whether you have any openings
  for work experience').
- The second paragraph should attempt to engage them by highlight-
  ing your interest in business along with some specific skills you can
  offer, such as knowledge of word processing or having a good telephone manner.
- Say in the letter whether you know anything about the company and
  how you found out about it (e.g. if friends or family work there) or
  whether you've read anything recently that was of interest or was
  relevant to your career prospects.

- Employers usually prefer typed letters, unless they specifically request one to be handwritten.

Whether you are applying for a position through an advertisement or just sending a speculative letter to a local company, you should do plenty of research on the employer. Having some information will help you tailor your CV for that particular company, and it will certainly be impressive if at an interview you show some knowledge of how the company works.

If you have an application form to fill in, follow the instructions carefully. Always complete forms neatly, using black ink. If your handwriting can be unclear, make sure that you take your time. You probably will not be asked to submit your CV as well, so always include evidence about your skills and interests in the statements in your application form.

It is imperative that you keep copies of all the letters, CVs and application forms you send off, not just so you can remember to whom you have applied but so that you have something to work from at an interview. You are bound to be asked to elaborate on things you have written about yourself, so do not say you have a skill or an interest if you cannot back it up.

Work experience interviews

Most of the tips from Chapter 6 are equally useful if you are going for a work experience interview. However, here are some additional pointers.

- Think through why you want the job, and in particular why you want to work for that organisation.
- Research the employer thoroughly before the interview. Look at their brochure and website.
- Plan in advance what you think your key selling points are for the employer and make sure you find an opportunity in the interview to get these across.
- Think up a few relevant questions to ask your interviewer at the end. You can demonstrate your preparation here by asking them about something you have read about the company recently, if appropriate.
- Remember to offer a nice, firm, confident handshake at the beginning and end of the interview.

Making the most of your work experience

You've gone through all of the above steps to secure yourself a work experience placement, but simply having spent some time in a business is not enough. You need to make sure you can demonstrate exactly what you have got from the experience. Here are some tips for making your experience really count.

1. **Keep a diary.** It will help you to remember what you did and, more importantly, what you learned from your experiences. You'll be able to draw on it when writing your personal statement and going to any interviews. Saying you have picked up new skills is almost useless without evidence, so writing things down will mean you can back up your claims later.

2. **Impress.** It isn't enough to just be there: make sure you are on time, presentable and enthusiastic. The employer will want to know that you value the experience so show them that you are taking it seriously.

3. **Be *seen* to be enthusiastic and professional.** Those around you are likely to be busy so you may need to get yourself noticed (in a good way!). If you have finished something, make sure you ask for something else to do, and ask questions to show that you are interested in what you are doing.

4. **Behave appropriately.** Being friendly is essential, but make sure you keep it professional. You are not there to make friends but to get valuable experience, so don't get drawn into office politics and remember you could need to call on any of your colleagues for help or as a reference at some point in the future.

5. **Be organised.** If you do all your work excellently but leave a trail of scrap paper everywhere you will be remembered for the wrong reasons.

6. **Network.** We're not talking about adding your new boss on Facebook (see number 4 – behave appropriately!); this is about making a good impression so that you can come back to people if it might be useful later on. You'll be surprised how often you'll need to call on the help of others for references or advice and those who get ahead seem to have networking down to a fine art. Before you leave, ask key staff if you could take their email addresses and if they would mind you contacting them if you need advice. If you think it would be useful to get more experience at the company or an internship (see below), ask your employer if there might be any opportunities coming up.

Internships

High Fliers Research conducted a study of 'The Graduate Market in 2012' and found that a third of graduates employed by the top 100 UK graduate recruiters in 2012 had already worked for their new employer while they were at university. This shows you just how much of an edge an internship can give you; in fact, some employers see summer internship programmes as an extended interview process, with top interns being offered jobs when they graduate. With this in mind, you should be checking what sort of support is available at the universities you are considering. Will they help you find a placement? What are the graduate employment figures like? Is there an opportunity to do a year in industry?

Internships come in all shapes and sizes. Some are over the summer holidays, while some are part-time alongside your studies, particularly after the second year of a course. It's never too early to start making links, as finding a work placement can often be half the battle. Opening up useful contacts by doing volunteering and work experience before university could prove very beneficial. Check with your local volunteering office or look at the following websites for information and ideas:

- Community Service Volunteers: www.csv.org.uk/find-us-near-you
- Do-it: www.do-it.org.uk
- Voluntary Service Overseas (VSO): www.vso.org.uk

3 | Choosing your course

You should remember that a degree in business, economics or management is not always a prerequisite for a specific role, nor is it a guarantee of a high-flying job. However, these courses provide an excellent foundation and may give you a head start in the world of business or finance over other graduates. Some courses are biased towards particular areas – such as econometrics, marketing or personnel. If you already have an interest in a particular area, look for courses where this will be drawn out and developed.

Prospects, the UK's leading provider of information, advice and guidance to students and graduates, estimates that 40% of vacancies advertised for graduates do not ask for a specific degree subject. Many potential employers are more interested in the class of a degree than its subject. If you do want to get into business but do not want to take business studies, it should not matter that much – as long as you do well in what you do and end up with a minimum of a 2.i degree. But if you are set on studying business, economics or management at degree level, read on – because there is a huge number of courses available and you will need to do some serious planning.

What to consider

You are allowed five choices on the UCAS form. The basic factors to consider when choosing your degree course are:

- the kind of business, economics, management, finance or related course you are looking for
- where you want to study
- your academic ability.

Going to university is an investment for your future and you need to squeeze the most out of your time there, so it pays to think hard about these points. They are all essential in helping you through the lengthy task of selecting what to study and where. Given the huge number of institutions offering business, economics and management courses, it is advisable to start by narrowing your options down to between 10 and 20. Once you have eliminated the bulk of the institutions and courses on offer, carry out your own detailed research.

- Contact your chosen universities or colleges and ask for their prospectuses (both official and alternative) and departmental brochures (if they exist) for more details. Remember that the universities' publications are promotional and may be selective about the information they provide.

- Visit the websites of the universities you are considering. These often contain more up-to-date information than the prospectuses.

- Attend university open days if you can, and talk to former or current students. Try to imagine whether you would be happy living for three or four years in that environment. You should consider issues such as whether you'd prefer to be on a campus or in a city, and whether there are facilities for you to pursue your other interests and hobbies.

- Talk to any people in business you know and ask for their views on the reputations of different universities and courses.

- Find out what academic criteria your shortlisted universities are looking for and be realistic about the grades you are expecting. Your teachers at school or college will be able to advise you on this.

- Make sure the course allows you to select any particular options you are interested in by thoroughly checking out what is available. The list can sometimes be mind-boggling! You will not always know what each option actually covers from its title, so read the department's own prospectus carefully and address any unanswered questions by contacting the admissions tutors directly.

- Think about whether or not you would like a course that includes an industrial placement. This can give you extremely valuable experience and is a great opportunity to make useful contacts for the future (see Chapter 2). Employers also like graduates who have had a practical placement. If you do choose such a course, it is well worth your while checking whose responsibility it is to find you a placement: does the university have a placement officer who will help you with this process, or is it entirely up to you to find something?

- Do you want to spend some time abroad? If you are doing a course that has some foreign language content, it might be possible to do a work placement in that country. This could be particularly valuable, as you would not only gain practical work experience but also improve your language skills, which could give you the edge when you come to look for a job after graduation.

- What are the computer and library facilities like at the university and the department to which you are applying? If you do not have your own computer, how many terminals are available for the number of students who are likely to be using them? This can be very important when you are rushing to finish an important project report! You should also check how readily available the books are that you require for the course – business and management books can be very expensive to buy.

- Try to find out about the reputation of the academic staff. If you are going to be taking a business and management degree, you might prefer to be taught by academics who have some experience of business themselves. Use the internet to find out what experience they have and what they've published.

League tables

When you are trying to select your five university choices, you may find university league tables helpful, as they will give you an indication of how a university or a course is regarded. A word of warning though – there are no official rankings of universities. The tables are normally compiled by the national newspapers and are based on a whole range of criteria. No two league tables will rank each university in the same way, nor will they produce the same results. However, they are a useful source of information, and might be one of the resources you use when making your choices. The *Guardian* newspaper, in its 2013 tables (www.guardian.co.uk/education/universityguide) ranked the top 10 universities in the UK as shown in Table 1.

Table 1 Top 10 universities in the UK

Rank	University
1	Cambridge
2	Oxford
3	LSE
4	St Andrews
5	Warwick
6	UCL
7=	Durham
7=	Lancaster
9	Bath
10	Exeter

Source: The *Guardian* 2013, www.guardian.co.uk/education/universityguide; © Guardian News and Media Limited

Table 2 shows the *Guardian*'s 2013 rankings for economics courses, while Table 3 shows their rankings for business and management courses.

Table 2 Top 10 economics courses

Rank	University
1	Oxford
2	LSE
3	Durham
4	Warwick
5	Cambridge
6	Kent
7=	Dundee
7=	Surrey
9	UCL
10=	Edinburgh
10=	Heriot-Watt

Source: The *Guardian* 2013, www.guardian.co.uk/education/universityguide; © Guardian News and Media Limited

Table 3 Top 10 business and management courses

Rank	University
1	Oxford
2	City
3	Warwick
4	Bristol
5	St Andrews
6	Bath
7	Loughborough
8	Strathclyde
9=	Glasgow
9=	LSE

Source: The *Guardian* 2013, www.guardian.co.uk/education/universityguide; © Guardian News and Media Limited

Note that these rankings include a number of areas of assessment, some of which might not be relevant to you. The *Guardian*'s tables can be reordered on the website by clicking on the category that you think is most important. For example, you could look at the economics ranking ordered by the entrance grades of students being accepted onto the course (a good indication of the quality of the students), as in Table 4. Other league tables that you might find useful include those produced by *The Times* (www.thetimes.co.uk/gooduniversityguide) and the Complete University Guide (www.thecompleteuniversityguide.co.uk).

You could also look, for example, at the ranking by job prospects, based on the destinations of graduates six months after graduating, as in Table 5.

Table 4 Top ten economics courses based on entrance grades

Rank	University
1	Cambridge
2	Oxford
3	LSE
4	Warwick
5	UCL
6	Durham
7	St Andrews
8	Exeter
9	Bath
10	Bristol

Source: The *Guardian* 2013, www.guardian.co.uk/education/universityguide;
© Guardian News and Media Limited

Table 5 Top 10 universities ranked by job prospects

Rank	University
1	Imperial
2	Cambridge
3	LSE
4	UCL
5	Bath
6	Kings
7	Bristol
8=	Robert Gordon
8=	Durham
8=	Glasgow

Source: The *Guardian* 2013, www.guardian.co.uk/education/universityguide;
© Guardian News and Media Limited

Once you have thoroughly researched the options available, you should have a shortlist of universities that fulfil your criteria – the course that suits your needs, the right locations, and the ability to pursue your interests. From that, you can choose the top five places to put in your UCAS application.

Other rankings and statistics

The National Student Survey is a big questionnaire completed by graduates all over the UK. It's really useful as it gives you a student perspective on what life is like at any given university. Results are published only for departments with over 50% survey completion, and they can be viewed online at unistats.direct.gov.uk.

Universities check up on their students six months after they have graduated to see what proportion have found work, are continuing their
studies, are having a gap year or are unemployed. Graduate employ-
ability figures can also be viewed at unistats.direct.gov.uk. Make sure
you look at the full data, as the information in the league tables is just an
overview to give an indication of graduate prospects. The Unistats website also allows you to look at student breakdown (including the male to
female ratio), degree classifications, and how many UCAS points successful applicants came to the course with.

For those who want to dig a little deeper, you can always check out the
latest QAA (Quality Assurance Agency) report on a particular university.
This is the body that inspects universities and publishes findings on how
institutions manage the quality of their qualifications. See www.qaa.
ac.uk for more information.

The next section outlines an assortment of factors that might have
some bearing on where you would like to study. See which are relevant
to you and try to put them in order of importance.

Academic and career-related factors

Your academic ability

For the majority of students, their A level scores will be the deciding
criterion for selection. It is important to be realistic about the grades you
are heading for: do not be too pessimistic, but do not kid yourself about
your as-yet-undiscovered genius. Talk to your teachers for an accurate
picture of your predicted results. Some places specify particular grades
but will still take you on if you get the same point score. So, for example, if you are supposed to get BBB (which amounts to 3 × 100 = 300
points), then any combination that produces 300 points (i.e. ABC or
AAD) may be acceptable. However, you should not assume this and
should always check with the university of your choice.

Educational facilities

Is there a well-stocked and up-to-date business library nearby, or will
you have to fight other business and management students for the
materials? Check for access to computer terminals if you do not have
your own or if you might not have internet access in your room. If you
are taking a joint degree involving sciences or languages, make sure
there are facilities for your other subjects, such as science or language
laboratories. The facilities available will depend on the budget of an institution, and plentiful resources tend to attract better tutors.

Quality of teaching

This is difficult to establish without the benefit of an open day, but the Higher Education Funding Council for England, the Higher Education Funding Council for Wales, the Scottish Funding Council and the Department for Education and Learning of Northern Ireland have done the groundwork for you and have assessed the level of teaching across the UK already. Their findings are publicly available – see www.hefce. ac.uk, www.hefcw.ac.uk, www.sfc.ac.uk and www.delni.gov.uk.

Teaching quality can suffer if seminar or tutorial groups are too large, so try to compare group sizes for the same courses at different institutions.

Type of institution

There are essentially three types of degree-awarding institutions: the 'old' universities, the 'new' universities and the colleges of higher education. There are also some private universities.

The 'old' universities

Traditionally the more academic universities, usually with higher admission requirements, the old universities are well established, with good libraries and research facilities. They have a reputation for being resistant to change, but most have introduced modern elements into their degrees such as modular courses, an academic year split into two semesters and programmes such as Erasmus.

The 'new' universities

Before 1992, these institutions were polytechnics, institutes or colleges. They form a separate group because they tend to still hold true to the original polytechnic mission of vocational courses and strong ties with industry, typically through placements and work experience. Because of this there are a number of excellent business and management degree courses at new universities that are very well regarded and entry is highly competitive. Some are still looked down on by certain employers because of their generally lower academic entry requirements, but the new universities have a good name for flexible admissions and learning, modern approaches to their degrees and good pastoral care.

Colleges of higher education

These are sometimes specialist institutions that provide excellent facilities in their chosen fields, despite their size. They are sometimes affiliated to universities. This form of franchising means that the college buys the right to teach the degree, which the university will award provided that the course meets the standards set by the university.

Private universities

There are two private universities in the UK that have their own degree-awarding powers (the University of Buckingham, which started in the 1970s; and BPP University College, which opened in 2010). Private universities are not funded by the government and are free to set their own tuition fees. There are other private universities in the UK whose degrees are awarded by overseas universities.

Attractiveness to employers

Few employers will openly admit to giving preference to graduates from particular universities. Most are looking for high-quality degrees, often a 2.i or above, as an indication of strong academic ability. But, since students with higher A level grades have tended to go to the old universities, it is unsurprising that a large proportion of successful business-people come from traditional university backgrounds.

A bit of research you can do yourself is to find out how past students have fared in the employment market. Ask to look at the university's annual final destinations survey, which should be available from its careers service or the department itself.

Distance learning

The vast majority of students choose to study full time and complete their degrees in the shortest possible period. However, if you are a mature student or it would be more convenient to your circumstances, you might wish to explore the option of distance learning. According to the International Centre for Distance Learning, there are around 20 business and business-related distance learning degree courses that you can study in the UK. Such courses include the BA in Business Studies at the University of East London, where 'students can take a shorter or longer time to complete the degree according to their needs and inclination'. However, students are normally expected to study one or two modules at any one time and take a minimum of three years to complete all 18 units.

The Open University (OU) also offers a BA degree in Business Studies. There are no entry requirements for this degree, but the OU states that 'you must be suitably prepared for study at undergraduate level'.

Non-academic considerations

Location

While some students have a clear picture of where they want to study, others are fairly geographically mobile, preferring instead to concentrate on choosing the right degree course and then seeing where they end up. But university life is not going to be solely about academic study. It is truly a growing experience – educationally, socially, culturally – and besides, three or four years can really drag if you are not happy outside the lecture theatre. The course search tool on the UCAS website is a good starting point because you can begin your search by specifying the regions in the UK where you would like to study.

Finances

The cost of living is not the same across the UK, so you should consider whether you will be able to reach deeper into your pockets for rent or other fundamentals and entertainment if you are living in a big city or in the south.

Friends and family

Do you want to get away from them or stay as close as possible? While there can be advantages, financial at least, to living at home, you might prefer the challenge of looking after yourself and the opportunity to be completely independent. You could have deeply personal reasons for applying to a particular university, but it is not a good idea to go to an institution just because your best friend is studying there.

Accommodation

Do you want to live in halls of residence with other students, or in private housing that you might need to organise yourself and could be a considerable distance from your place of study? Most institutions have an accommodation officer who will help you find a suitable place to live; and many universities will guarantee a room in halls of residence to first-year students anyway. But you will probably have to fend for yourself at some stage, so check on the availability of student housing, the cost and the distance from the university. If your university is nearby, is there any point moving away from home?

Leisure and entertainment

Are you going to be spending much time in, for example, the sports centre, the theatre or student bars? How about university societies – is there one that allows you to indulge your existing hobbies or caters for those you have always dreamt of trying?

Case study

'I chose to study economics mainly because I really enjoyed it at A level. I really enjoyed the macroeconomics and maths aspects of the degree, but a lot of the economics taught at university is very theoretical, whereas I preferred it to be more practical and applicable to the real world. I didn't do an internship or industry placement, but lots of my friends did and it's one of the best ways to get into a banking or finance job after university, so I might have considered it if I'd known. Some banks even offer internships for first-year students. Surprisingly, A level Maths is considered more of a prerequisite for economics than A level Economics, so my first piece of advice to applicants would be to concentrate on your maths as it will give you more options when choosing an economics course. Secondly, I'd recommend that you start reading *The Economist*, the BBC Business Section, *The Financial Times*, etc. to get to grips with current economic stories and the language.'

Pritesh, BSc Economics graduate, University College London

Site and size

Many universities overcome the problems of urban versus rural and small versus large by locating their campuses on the edge of a major town (e.g. the University of Nottingham and the University of Kent) and centralising certain facilities and services to ensure safety, convenience and some sense of community, even on the largest and most widespread campus. But some students prefer to feel they are part of the local town or city community, rather than being isolated on an out-of-town site: the bigger single-campus universities might cover a larger area than some of the smaller multi-site institutions. And do not be put off by the expression 'multi-site' – individual sites are likely to be self-contained, so students do not have to travel to other sites too often.

Case study

'I chose a joint honours course as I genuinely didn't know which road to go down. I'd enjoyed both subjects at A level and wanted to keep my future options open.

'I liked being able to choose complementary modules from each discipline so I didn't get bored by just one subject. The major advantage I found was that my stronger discipline (business) pulled up my marks overall and it didn't matter so much that it turned out I was not as strong in the computer science side.

'Studying a joint degree gave me an insight into both subjects and potential careers. It also helped me to decide which direction to go in after I graduated. I really appreciated the flexibility in my final year which allowed me to choose modules from each degree that complemented each other and to tailor a course which reflected my own strengths and interests. My only regret is that I chose a joint degree that wasn't equally weighted (it was two-thirds computer science), especially as business proved to be my stronger area.'

Leah, joint honours graduate in Computer Science with Business Management, University of Birmingham

4| The UCAS application

The following advice should help you complete your UCAS application. More specific advice on filling in your application is given in *How to Complete Your UCAS Application: 2014 entry* (Trotman Publishing, May 2013), which is updated annually (see Chapter 11).

The application

The UCAS application is completed on the UCAS website. There are six sections to complete.

1. **Personal information.** Your name, address, nationality, and how the course is going to be funded. This should be the easiest part of the form to complete, but you need to read the instructions carefully to avoid making mistakes.
2. **Student finance.** If you are planning to apply for student finance, you can complete this section to make your finance application easier. (UCAS will share your information, to make the two processes more streamlined.)
3. **Your choices of university.** You are allowed to choose five courses. Again, pay particular attention to the course codes and university codes, and ensure that all of the required information (where you intend to live, to which campus you are applying, etc.) is included.
4. **Education.** This means your examination results, where you have studied, and any examinations to be sat.
5. **Employment.** If you have had gaps in your education because you were in employment, you need to give the details here.
6. **Personal statement.** See Chapter 5 for more about this.

Once you have completed all of these sections, your referee will add his or her comments about your suitability for your chosen courses. Your referee is normally someone at your school or college (such as a housemaster or head of sixth form), but for applicants who are not at school, this might be an employer (see Chapter 7).

Suggested timescale

Here is a suggested timescale to help you fill in the UCAS application to the best of your ability.

Year 12

May/June: Do some serious thinking. Get ideas from friends, relatives, teachers, books, etc. If possible, visit some campuses before you go away anywhere during the summer.

June/July: Make a shortlist of your courses.

August: Get your hands on some copies of the official and alternative (student-written) prospectuses, and departmental brochures for extra detail. They can usually be found in school or college libraries, but all the information can also be found by looking at university websites.

Year 13

September: Complete your application online and submit it to UCAS via a referee. It will be accepted from 1 September onwards.

15 October: Deadline for applying for places at Oxford or Cambridge.

November: Universities hold their open days and sometimes interviews. Entrance examinations for some Oxford and Cambridge courses.

15 January: Deadline for submitting your application to UCAS. (Late applications may be considered, but your chances are limited since some of the places will have already gone.)

April: Universities begin to make their decisions and offers will be sent directly to you. If you are rejected by all of your choices, you can use UCAS Extra to look at other universities.

15 May: You must tell UCAS which offer you have accepted firmly and which one is your backup. (The deadline is two weeks after the final decision you receive, if this falls earlier.)

Spring: Fill out yet more forms – this time for fees and student loans. You can get these from your school, college or local authority.

Summer: Sit your exams and wait for your results. If you are sitting exams in the UK (e.g. A level, Scottish Highers, International Baccalaureate), UCAS and your universities will receive your results automatically. When the results are published, UCAS will get in touch and tell you whether your chosen universities have confirmed your conditional offers. For a full list of qualifications that UCAS receives, see the UCAS website. If you are taking an examination that UCAS does not receive or you are sitting exams outside the UK, you may need to send your results to your universities yourself. Your school or college should be able to help you with this and the university admissions team can tell you what you need to do.

Do not be too disappointed if you have not got into your chosen institution; just get in touch with your school/college or careers office and wait until Clearing begins in mid-August, when all remaining places are filled. You will be sent instructions on Clearing automatically, but it is up to you to get hold of the published lists of available places and to contact the universities directly. If you have done better than expected, you can use the Adjustment system to look for universities that require higher grades (see Chapter 8).

Entrance examinations

If you are applying to Oxford or Cambridge universities, you will have to sit an extra entrance examination. Details of these can be found in *Getting into Oxford & Cambridge: 2014 entry* (Trotman Publishing, 2013). The London School of Economics (LSE) also sets an entrance test for some candidates whose educational background is non-standard; for example, if they have studied on an Access course. Other universities may be introducing extra tests in the future, and you should check on the UCAS website or with the university to find out whether you will need to sit one. These tests are used to further differentiate between students, as predicted A level grades are often not enough to separate candidates. Oxford and Cambridge use Thinking Skills Assessment (TSA) scores and A level results to decide whether or not to call you for interview. A serious candidate would make sure they visit the appropriate website (listed below) to ensure that they are prepared and know what to expect.

The TSA is required by Oxford University (if you take economics and management or philosophy, politics and economics (PPE)) and by Cambridge University (if you take economics).

TSA Oxford

- The test is taken in early November.
- It consists of 50 multiple-choice questions to be completed in 90 minutes and a 30-minute essay from a choice of three questions.
- Details and practice papers can be found at www.admissionstests. cambridgeassessment.org.uk/adt/tsaoxford.

TSA Cambridge

- The test is taken at the interview.
- It consists of 50 questions to be completed in 90 minutes.
- Details and practice papers can be found at www.admissionstests. cambridgeassessment.org.uk/adt/tsacambridge.

LSE

- Candidates are informed between December and February in the academic year of application if they are required to sit the test.
- It consists of a three-hour written paper testing English, comprehension and mathematics.
- Details and practice papers can be found at www2.lse.ac.uk/study/ undergraduate/howToApply/entranceExam.aspx.

Sample Oxford TSA paper

The questions below were taken from a past paper.

Section 1

Splashford Swimming Pool charges £2 per session for adults and £1 for children.

Also available is a Family Swimcard. At a cost of £50, the Family Swimcard allows unlimited use of the pool for one year for two adults and up to three children. For larger families, every additional child must pay half the children's rate each time.

Mr and Mrs Teal and their four children are keen swimmers. They used their Swimcard when the family went swimming 40 times last year.

How much did the Swimcard save the Teal family last year?

A   £50
B   £190
C   £230
D   £250
E   £270

The United States attempts to reduce the supply of illegal drugs by intercepting shipments and eradicating illegal crops. Despite these efforts, illegal drugs are still readily available, because growers, for example those in Colombia, move to different areas and plant smaller plots that are harder to find. So more effort should be made to reduce demand. This does not simply mean reducing the total number of people using illegal drugs. Because the important task is to cut consumption by heavy users, drug-dependent criminals in the country's jails should be treated for their addiction. In this way drug-related social problems can be reduced.

Which one of the following, if true, most strengthens the above argument?

A The price of drugs has not fallen despite efforts to reduce their supply.
B Statistics show that many crops of illegal drugs in Colombia have been eradicated.
C Most of the drug users in US jails do not want treatment for their drug addiction.
D Heavy drug users are responsible for committing most of the drug-related crime.
E The majority of the US public are in favour of rehabilitating prisoners who are drug users.

Section 2

'Printing and the telephone were truly revolutionary inventions. All the internet brings is a difference in scale.' Is that true?

If two reasonable people claim the same fact as evidence for opposing conclusions, does it follow that it can't actually be evidence for either?

Sample Cambridge TSA paper

School examination results in England this year reinforce the trend in improving pass rates. There is, however, no other evidence of improvements in school leavers' abilities – such as the data coming from employers or universities. One can reasonably conclude, therefore, that teachers are simply succeeding in coaching their pupils better for examinations than in previous years.

Which one of the following is an underlying assumption of the above argument?

A School examination results are a reliable indicator of pupils' abilities.
B The level of difficulty of examinations has not been falling.
C Employers' expectations of school leavers are unrealistic.

D Teachers in previous years did not attempt to coach pupils for examinations.
E Abilities of school pupils vary from year to year.

Ever since Uranus was discovered in 1781, astronomers have thought there might be more planets to be discovered in the Solar System. Because of small deviations in the orbits of Uranus and Neptune – deviations which would occur if another planet existed – some astronomers think there must be an undiscovered planet – Planet X. But the search for Planet X is futile, because these deviations would occur if the orbits had been wrongly pre-dicted. Since Uranus and Neptune take many decades to circle the sun, astronomers must rely on old data in order to calculate their orbits. If this data is inaccurate, the calculated orbits are wrong. If the calculated orbits are wrong, Uranus and Neptune will deviate from them even if there is no Planet X.

Which of the following is the best statement of the flaw in the argument above?

A From the fact that the old data is inaccurate, it cannot be inferred that the calculated orbits are wrong.
B From the fact that the data about the orbits is old, it cannot be inferred that it is inaccurate.
C From the fact that deviations occur which would occur if Planet X existed, it cannot be inferred that Planet X exists.
D From the fact that the calculated orbits are wrong, it cannot be inferred that Uranus and Neptune will deviate from them.
E From the fact that Planet X has not been discovered, it cannot be inferred that the search for it is futile.

The roller coaster at Blue Top Towers Park runs continuously from 10.00am to 6.00pm during the week and from 9.00am to 7.00pm at weekends.

Each ride lasts for 3 minutes.

It can take up to 5 minutes to unload and reload between rides at busy periods, but even when the park is quiet there is a 2-minute gap between the end of one ride and the beginning of the next.

What is the maximum number of rides there can be in one day?
A   60
B   75
C   96
D   120
E   200

Taken from the specimen papers available on the Cambridge Assessment website (www.admissionstests.cambridgeassessment.org.uk). Reprinted by permission of the University of Cambridge Local Examinations Syndicate.

Answers to Section 1 questions from the Oxford TSA: D, D

Answers to Cambridge TSA questions: B, B, D

Taking a gap year

Most admissions tutors are happy for students to take a gap year in between their final year at school or college and the start of university. Of course, whether or not your gap year enhances and strengthens your application depends on what your gap year plans entail.

There are two application routes for students taking gap years. One option is for students to apply for deferred entry – that is, applying in the final year of the A level course for entry a year later. So, a student sitting A levels in June 2013 would apply for entry in September/October 2014, not 2013. Alternatively, students can apply at the start of the gap year, once their A level results are known.

There are advantages in both routes, depending on your plans and A level grades.

Deferred entry

With deferred entry:

- you will know where you are going to study in August, before you start your gap year
- you will not need to interrupt your gap year plans for interviews
- if you are unsuccessful in getting offers from your chosen universities or courses, you can reapply during the gap year.

Applying during the gap year

If you apply during the gap year:

- you will know your examination grades, so you can target your application much more effectively
- if your school is not predicting high grades but you feel confident in achieving higher than the predictions, you do not run the risk of being rejected based on the predictions.

Whichever route you take, it is important to plan the gap year properly so that it is clear to the universities that you (and they) will benefit from it.

The point of the gap year is to gain work or life experience, maturity and independence, or to earn money to help fund your studies. Admissions tutors are not going to be impressed with a gap year that involves watching TV and sleeping simply because you worked hard at your A levels and feel like a break from study.

Here is an excerpt from a personal statement:

> *'I am going to take a gap year during which I hope to travel and to gain more work experience.'*

This is not going to convince the admissions tutors that (a) you have actually made any plans at all, or (b) this is a year that is likely to help you develop or bring new skills and ideas onto their courses.

A better version might be:

> *'During my gap year, I have arranged a placement with a local travel agent, where I will be assisting with planning group tours to various European countries. I hope that this will help me to under-stand more about how a company sets its prices and its budgets, particularly in a field where prices and exchange rates fluctuate on a day-to-day basis. The work experience will also be useful because, from March, I will be travelling in Asia, visiting India, Thailand, Vietnam and Cambodia. In Cambodia, I have arranged to teach English in an orphanage for one month. To fund this, I will be working in the evenings in a local restaurant while on my work placement with the travel company.'*

This is much more impressive because the candidate has linked what she will do to her future degree course (business studies), and it is clear that she has thought carefully about what she will do during the year.

Students often use phrases such as 'I hope to . . .' when 'I have arranged . . .' or 'I have planned . . .' are more likely to convince the university selectors that they are going to use the year usefully.

Gap year plans

Gap year plans do not have to involve travel to distant countries (although this is a useful and enjoyable thing to do). There are many other fulfilling ways of using your 12 months. The important thing is to be able to justify the plans either at the interview or in your personal statement. Other things you might consider include:

- internships (see Chapter 2)
- full- or part-time employment to earn money or to gain experience
- full- or part-time courses, such as IT, art, languages or practical skills
- helping with a university research project
- voluntary or charity work
- community projects.

If you are not sure whether your chosen university will be happy for you to take a gap year, contact it at the start of your final year of A levels and ask. Many universities also include a statement of their gap year policy on their websites.

Replies from the universities

After your application has been assessed by the university, you will receive a response. You can also follow the progress of your application using the online Track facility on the UCAS website. You will receive one of three possible responses from each university:

1. a conditional offer
2. an unconditional offer
3. a rejection.

If you receive a conditional offer, you will be told what you need to achieve in your A levels. This could be in grade terms, for example AAB (and the university might specify a particular grade in a particular subject – AAB with an A in economics), or in UCAS tariff points (for example 300 points from three A levels – see Chapter 11). Unconditional offers can be given to students who have already sat their A levels, such as gap-year students applying post-results. Rejection means that you have been unsuccessful in your application to that university.

If you receive five rejections, then you can enter the UCAS Extra scheme, through which you can make one additional choice at a time. You may also use UCAS Extra if you change your mind about the courses you have applied for and you decline all the offers you are holding. Be careful when doing this: read the information in Chapter 8 on using Extra.

Once you have received responses from all five universities, you will need to make your choice of the university offer you wish to accept. This is called your firm choice. You can also choose an insurance offer, which is effectively a second choice with a lower grade requirement. UCAS will give you a deadline of about a month to make this decision from the date when you receive your fifth response. You may have a different deadline to your friends so make sure you know what your own deadline is by checking the UCAS Track service.

5 | The personal statement

The most important part of your UCAS application is the personal statement. This is where you have 47 lines (or 4,000 characters including spaces, whichever you use first) to convince the five universities you are applying to that:

- you are serious about wanting to study on the course
- you have researched the options available to you for the degree course and for your future career
- you are suitable for the course
- you are a well-rounded individual who can contribute to the life of the university.

'Economics is a subject based on analysis and mathematics, so I like it when students with a science background apply. I do not give preference to students who have economics at A level over those who don't because I know that not all schools offer it. But I am very interested in students who have studied sciences, and I am less likely to offer places to students without at least AS mathematics, unless they have studied a science. Apart from that, I like to see breadth in the A level choice. I will consider students who are studying one 'non-preferred' subject (such as art or media studies) but not two out of the three A levels.'

An admissions tutor for economics

Before you start to write your personal statement, you need to finalise your choice of courses. Why? Because the personal statement has to convince an admissions tutor at a university that you are a serious applicant. It is important to remember that you write one personal statement that is read by all five universities to which you are applying. The people reading the personal statement do not know which other universities you are applying to, or for what courses. All they will be assessing is whether your personal statement is applicable for their particular course.

If an admissions tutor is selecting students for an economics degree course, he or she will be looking for personal statements that address economics; if an admissions tutor is selecting students to study business studies, he or she will be expecting to read about business-related issues. It is important, therefore, to ensure that there is as much compatibility between your five choices as possible, otherwise you run the risk of being rejected by all of them.

'Applicants need to remember that everything I know about them, everything that gives me an idea about whether I can consider them for a place or not, is contained in the few pages of the UCAS application, and so they need to demonstrate (preferably with examples, anecdotes or evidence) that they have researched my course and that they have a good reason for studying management. With the best will in the world, I cannot offer places to students who come across as delightful and interesting people from what I read in their personal statements and references if there is no convincing evidence that they have thought seriously about studying management.

'What can they do to convince me? Write about books they have read, work experience they have done, news items about business or management that interest them, how their A levels relate to a career in management – there is no "right" way to do this, but the wrong way to go about convincing me is to cram the personal statement full of very general statements rather than focusing on specifics.'

An admissions tutor for management

Applying for more than one course at the same university?

The UCAS system allows you to apply for more than one course at a particular university. But beware: applying for two courses at the same institution does not double your chances of studying there. As an example, take the case of a student who is desperate to study at Barton University. She decides to apply for both the joint honours economics and mathematics and the single honours economics courses. What she is unaware of is that the admissions tutor for economics will look at her application for the two courses, and that the admissions tutor for mathematics will look at the application for the mathematics and economics course. Our applicant's main interest is economics, so her personal statement emphasises this, but it also devotes one paragraph to mathematics. The economics admissions tutor reading the personal statement will judge it on how it addresses economics, so he or she will either make offers for both courses or reject the student for both courses. The mathematics admissions tutor will be looking for evidence of an interest in mathematics, so he or she will probably reject the student for the mathematics and economics course because it is too focused on economics. By trying to increase her probability of getting into Barton University, our applicant may in fact reduce her chances because her personal statement is neither focused enough on economics, nor is it specific enough about mathematics to satisfy the mathematics department. So bear the following in mind.

- **Rule Number 4.** When writing the personal statement, try to imagine how it will come across to each of the departments to which you are applying. Don't try to write something too general just so you have the luxury of applying to a wider range of courses.

The structure of the personal statement

There is no one formula for a perfect personal statement. It is called a personal statement because it should reflect your interests and achievements. However, as a general guideline, the personal statement should cover four areas:

1. why you have chosen the course
2. how you have investigated whether the course is suitable for you
3. what makes you stand out from your peers
4. other information relevant to the application; for example, if you are taking a gap year, what you will be doing during that year.

Why you have chosen the course

This could include:

- what first interested you in economics, business or management; for example, watching the news about the failure of a bank, an article in a newspaper about globalisation, or personal experience, such as work experience or the family business
- a particular career plan
- a combination of your particular interests and academic skills.

How you have investigated whether the course is suitable for you

This could include:

- books, periodicals or websites that you have read
- work experience (see Chapter 2)
- lectures that you have attended
- skills that you have gained from your A levels.

What makes you stand out from your peers

This could include:

- academic achievements; for example, prizes or awards
- extracurricular activities and achievements
- responsibilities; for example as school prefect, head of house, captain of netball team, or voluntary or charity work
- evidence of teamwork; for example, sports teams, Duke of Edinburgh Award expeditions, or part-time jobs
- travel.

Other information relevant to the application

This could include:

- gap year plans
- personal circumstances; for example, it might be necessary for you to study in your home city because of the need to help care for a disabled parent.

'My university probably has more applicants per place for economics than any other in the country, and it amuses me to hear the rumours that fly around among students about why we reject people. The most popular rumour is that we reject a student if they are applying to Oxford or Cambridge because we believe that they are not serious about us. What they don't understand is that I do not know where else they are applying to. I see my institution's name on the form, and the student's details and personal statement. However, I will reject someone if their personal statement does not address the issues that we ask them to write about – the information we require is made very clear on our website. So if a student has written a personal statement that is clearly aimed at another course, they may well be rejected.'

An admissions tutor for economics

Sample personal statement 1 (character count: 1,605)

I have chosen to study management at university because I want to run a business in the future, and management skills will be very important for this. I first became interested in management because my father runs a company and so I was able to see how important this aspect of the business is.

Last summer, I spent two weeks shadowing a department manager in a local company, and I gained an insight into the skills required to be a successful manager. In particular, I observed the need for good communication skills. I enjoy reading *The Economist* and the business sections of the national newspapers.

I am studying mathematics, economics and physics at A level. Mathematics is useful because it helps me to understand balance sheets and share prices, which are essential skills for a successful businessman. Economics has taught me how a company's success depends on how it adapts to the way the market is performing, and how it copes with fluctuations in the global economy. Physics teaches me how to be analytical and how to solve problems.

At school, I am captain of the 1st XV rugby team. This requires the ability to show leadership qualities and to manage people. It also allows me to get rid of stress. I play the trombone in the school orchestra, which involves teamwork and manual dexterity. I like reading, going to the cinema, and photography. I also have a passion for opera. On Saturdays, I work at the local Louisiana Fried Turkey fast-food restaurant, and so I have gained excellent communication and teamwork skills. In my gap year I hope to travel and to gain more work experience.

Points raised by sample personal statement 1

- It is too short, at fewer than 2,000 characters (remember the maximum is 4,000 characters). You should aim to use the full amount of space available.
- Although the candidate has addressed all of the relevant issues, there is a lack of detail. It is too general and tells us very little about the candidate.
- It is not very personal.

An admissions tutor's comments on sample personal statement 1

'I have chosen to study management at university because I want to run a business in the future, and management skills will be very important for this.' (1) 'I first became interested in management because my father runs a company' (2) 'and so I was able to see how important this aspect of the business is.' (3)

1. Why are management skills important? – give an example of a situation you have seen, discussed or read about that illustrates this.
2. Give details of the company – what does it do? Who does it trade with?
3. An example would add detail to this section – perhaps recount an incident that shows the importance of a good management structure, or about the need to delegate.

'Last summer, I spent two weeks shadowing a department manager' (4) 'in a local company,' 'and I gained an insight into the skills required to be a successful manager. In particular, I observed the need for good communication skills.' (5) 'I enjoy reading The Economist *and the business sections of the national newspapers.' (6)*

4. Which department? What did the company do? How big was it? You could write something along the lines of '. . . which manufactured electric motors to be used in agricultural settings . . .' This might well stimulate an interesting discussion at the interview stage.
5. Give an example, such as 'As an example of this, I remember one occasion when a local farmer needed us to adapt one of the products to . . .'
6. Also, give an example that relates to something you have studied at A level. This should be the strongest and longest section of the personal statement. I want to know much more about what the applicant gained from the work experience and why it has convinced him/her that my course is the right one.

'I am studying mathematics, economics and physics at A level. Mathematics is useful because it helps me to understand balance sheets and share prices, which are essential skills for a successful businessman. Economics has taught me how a company's success depends on how it adapts to the way the market is performing, and how it copes with fluctuations in the global economy. Physics teaches me how to be analytical and how to solve problems.' (7)

7. This is OK, but could do with links between what the applicant has studied at A level and what he/she has discovered about business

and management in the real world through reading and work experience.

'At school, I am captain of the 1st XV rugby team. This requires the ability to show leadership qualities and to manage people. It also allows me to get rid of stress. I play the trombone in the school orchestra, which involves teamwork and manual dexterity. I like reading, going to the cinema, and photography. I also have a passion for opera. On Saturdays, I work at the local Louisiana Fried Turkey fast-food restaurant, and so I have gained excellent communication and teamwork skills. In my gap year I hope to travel and to gain more work experience.' (8)

8. This sentence could be more detailed – rather than 'hope to travel', I would like to see something more definite – 'I have arranged to . . .' I want to be reassured that the applicant is going to use the gap year wisely and to benefit from it.

Adding the extra information requested by this admissions tutor would add detail, make it more interesting for him to read (so he is more likely to want to meet the student), demonstrate that the student is interested enough in the subject to be thinking about links between his studies and his experiences, and bring the statement up to the required length.

So remember the following.

* **Rule Number 5.** Details turn an easily forgettable personal statement into something that will stand out from the rest.

Links and connections

As you will have noticed from the previous example, a good way to show that you have thought about the subject and the course is to make links and connections between your different areas of research and preparation. You could think about linking:

* aspects of your A level subjects with things you will study on the course
* qualities necessary for success in this field with your own experiences; for example, captaining a school team or organising a school event
* an article that you read with something that you observed in your work experience.

You could start this process by making lists, or diagrammatically, as in Figure 2.

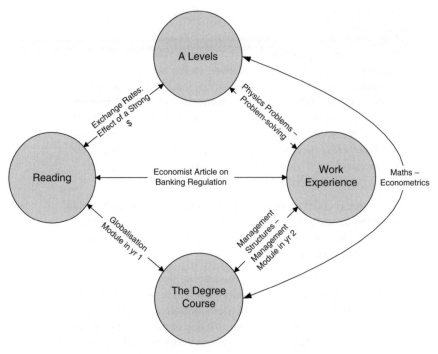

Figure 2 Making links between study and experience

How to get started on the personal statement

How **not** to get started on your personal statement would be to . . .

- plan how you are going to say all you want in exactly 47 lines
- write down your ideas in perfectly formed sentences, suitable for the final version
- download sample personal statements from the internet and try to adapt them.

A better strategy is to start by making lists of anything that you think is relevant to your application, then to begin organising them into sections. Your personal statement could include some of the following points.

'My interest in the subject began because of . . .

- a newspaper article I read
- a book I read
- a news item
- my work experience
- my parents' work
- my A level subjects.'

'I have researched this subject by . . .

- reading books
- reading *The Financial Times*
- reading *The Economist*
- reading *Business Week*
- work experience
- attending lectures
- talking to . . .
- downloading a podcast of a university lecture on iTunesU.'

'My work experience taught me . . .

- that the qualities a good manager/accountant/businessman/economist needs are . . .
- how to relate what I have been taught in A level economics to real-life situations . . .
- the importance of teamwork/accuracy/decision making . . .'

Other relevant points are given below.

- 'My A level subjects are useful because . . .'
- 'My Saturday job is useful because . . .'
- 'My role as school prefect has taught me . . .'
- 'Being captain of the 1st XV (or netball, or leader of the orchestra, or . . .) has taught me . . .'
- 'During my gap year I have arranged to . . .'
- 'I was awarded first prize for . . .'

Only when you have the ideas structured into some sort of logical order should you start to write full sentences and to link the points. Which leads to the next rule.

- **Rule Number 6.** Always use examples and evidence to illustrate the points you are making in the personal statement.

Language

Given the limit on the number of characters (4,000) that make up the personal statement, it is important to make every sentence count, and not to waste space with passages that are at best too general and at worst meaningless. You should use clear, simple English and make sure that the content of what you are writing impresses the selectors, rather than trying to win them over with flowery, overcomplicated phrases.

> *'I was privileged to be able to undertake some work experience with a well-known high-street bank where I was able to see the benefit of having the ability to be confident with information technology.'*
>
> **– 199 characters**

This could be rewritten as:

> *'My three weeks' work placement at HSBC showed me the importance of being proficient in using spreadsheets.'*
>
> **– 106 characters**

Similarly:

> *'I was honoured to be able to captain my school Under–14, Under–15, Second XV and First XV rugby sides, and from this I learnt how to be an effective leader and an excellent communicator.'*
>
> **– 186 characters**

. . . could be rewritten as:

> *'Captaining my school 1st XV taught me the importance of strong leadership and communication skills.'*
>
> **– 99 characters**

Phrases to avoid include the following.

- 'I was honoured to be . . .'
- 'I was privileged to . . .'
- 'From an early age . . .'
- 'It has always been my dream to . . .'

Hence . . .

- **Rule Number 7.** Every word counts, so do not waste space by using overcomplicated language or words that are designed to impress.

Sample personal statement 2 was written by an international student who was subsequently offered places by all five of her chosen universities. It is very individual in style, and reflects the student's interest and achievements in mathematics, but, throughout, she relates mathematics to economics. Thus, she is able to demonstrate how one of her key strengths will be relevant to her university studies.

Sample personal statement 2 (character count: 3,958)

If mathematics uses numbers and symbols to convey ideas and concepts, and social sciences make use of language to express hypotheses, economics is something in between, since it requires not only the logical analysis of mathematics to address theoretical problems but also the clarity of language to convert its theoretical perspectives into real-world applications. It is this special feature of economics that initially drew my interest to the subject.

To understand more about economic models, I read 'Fundamental Methods of Mathematical Economics' by Alpha Chiang. Although the methods and models described are at their simplest forms and not yet comprehensive enough to depict real-world problems, I was surprised to see how powerful mathematics can be in economics when different mathematical techniques, from the simple simultaneous equations and calculus that I studied in my A level maths to complicated series expansions that I have not yet encountered, were employed in various micro and macro models to solve problems such as optimisation or national income. Knowing how powerful mathematics can be in economics, I'm also aware of its limitations. A model can be internally consistent but its subject matter, people, are capricious. This makes economic models sometimes unable to forecast events such as the current recession. As such, economics is not independent of human psychology and we cannot study the subject in a vacuum.

In work-shadowing at the Finance Department of my province this summer, I found that statistics and econometrics in Vietnam have only been developed in the last two years. Indeed, our CPI (consumer price index) is calculated without weightings taken into account. This type of inaccuracy is quite common in Vietnam and draws a misleading picture of the economy's performance. I would like to pursue econometrics at university to help develop this branch of economics in my country. I hope that with my contribution, no matter how small, Vietnam can produce reliable statistics and test economic policies on its own in the near future.

Coming from a developing nation, I cannot but have a strong interest in development economics. 'Globalization and its Discontents' by Joseph Stiglitz has changed my view about the role of international economic institutions, particularly of the IMF, in promoting economic welfare and stability. According to the author, the IMF is notorious in setting many conditions for its loans, and sometimes the loans made are insufficient or inefficient to help countries get out of predicaments. This also applies to Vietnam, when the IMF cut its loans for our poverty reduction programme in the three years to 2007, arguing that our central banks did not meet four of five criteria to qualify for the funding source. Having said that, since the book is eight years old, it fails to appreciate the efforts of the institution to make its fund more available to countries in need in recent years.

Outside class, I enjoy solving maths puzzles and won a gold medal for the Senior Maths Challenge together with a distinction in the British Maths Olympiad. In Vietnam, I was also awarded a

4th prize in the Provincial Maths Competition for 11th grade gifted students when I was in my 10th grade, and the first prize in a Maths Contest for the 9th grade gifted students. In economics, I attended Target 2.0 last year. My group was in charge of the 'Cost and Price' section. This required dealing with figures such as commodity prices, input and output costs of firms, etc. and one must be able to choose the related data to make the rate decisions.

I enjoy reading novels in my free time. My favourite book is 'Crime and Punishment'. Through reading, I have developed sympathy and moral concern towards the people and communities around me. I believe this to be an important virtue in an economist, because to understand people is the first condition for one to apply economics for the good of society.

General tips

- Keep a copy of your personal statement so you can remind yourself of all the wonderful things you said about yourself, should you be called for interview!
- Print off a copy of your application to remind yourself of what you have said. Before submitting it, also ensure you check your application through very carefully for careless errors that are harder to see on screen.

And remember the seven rules for a successful application.

1. Research the course content.
2. Research the entrance requirements.
3. Find out your grade predictions.
4. Ensure your personal statement focuses on the course but remember to imagine how it will come across to each of the departments to which you are applying.
5. Include sufficient detail in the personal statement to make it stand out.
6. Illustrate your points with examples and evidence.
7. Every word in a personal statement counts, so don't use complicated language just to impress the admissions tutor.

6 | Succeeding at interview

Some universities will want to interview prospective students before making their final decisions (Oxford and Cambridge will almost always interview before offering a place). Interviews need not be as daunting as you fear. They are designed to help the people asking the questions to find out as much about you as they can. Treat the experience positively as a chance to put yourself across well, rather than as an obstacle course designed to catch you out.

If you are invited for an interview, here are some points to bear in mind.

- Remember that if you shine in your interview and impress the admissions staff, they may drop their grades slightly and make you a lower offer.
- It is important to make eye contact and use confident body language.
- Interviewers are more interested in what you know than what you do not. If you are asked a question you do not know the answer to, say so. Waffling simply wastes time and lets you down. To lie, of course, is even worse – especially for anyone hoping to demonstrate the integrity and honesty suited to a business career.
- Remember: your future tutor might be among the people interviewing you, so it's important to be polite.
- Enthusiasm, a strong commitment to your subject and, above all, a willingness to learn are extremely important attitudes to convey.
- An ability to think on your feet is vital . . . another prerequisite for a career in business or management. Pre-learned answers never work. Putting forward an answer using examples and factual knowledge to reinforce your points will impress interviewers far more. Essential preparation includes revision of the personal statement on your UCAS application, so do not include anything in your UCAS application that you are not prepared to speak about at interview.
- Questions may well be asked about your extracurricular activities. This is often a tactic designed to put you at your ease and to find out about the sort of person you are; therefore, your answers should be thorough and enthusiastic.
- At the end of the interview, you will probably be asked whether there is anything you would like to ask your interviewer. If you have nothing to ask, then say that your interview has covered everything you thought of. It is sensible, however, to have up your sleeve one

or two questions of a serious kind – to do with the course, the tuition and so on. However, it is not wise to ask anything that you could and should have found out from the prospectus, such as 'what accommodation do you offer to first-year students?'

- Above all, end on a positive note, and remember to smile! Make them remember you when they review their list of 20 or more candidates at the end of the day.

Preparation for an interview

Preparation for an interview should be an intensification of the work you are already doing outside class for your A level courses. Interviewers will be looking for evidence of an academic interest and commitment that extends beyond the classroom. They will also be looking for an ability to apply the theories and methods that you have been learning in your A level courses to the real world.

Whichever resources you use, this advice assumes that you will be taking a single honours business or management degree, but if you have chosen a joint or combined honours course you will have to prepare yourself for questions on those other subjects as well.

Either way, the interview is a chance for you to demonstrate knowledge of, commitment to and enthusiasm for business. The only way to do this is to be extremely well informed. Interviewers will want to know your reasons for wishing to study business. It is important to be aware of the many aspects of business, e.g. marketing, finance, personnel, and be clear about the differences between the various functions.

Newspapers and magazines

As an A level student, you should already be reading a quality newspaper every day. Before your interview, it is vital that you are aware of current affairs related to the course for which you are being interviewed. *The Financial Times* will give you a good grasp of business, as will reading the business sections of the other broadsheets. You should also keep up to date with current affairs in general.

Magazines are another important source of comment on current issues and deeper analysis. *The Economist* is a popular example, but you might also find it helpful to pick up a more specialist magazine such as *Talk Business*. Reading professionally written articles keeps you well informed about current events and gives you the chance to see how the vocabulary and language of business are used to communicate news and views. Magazines such as *Enterprise* and *HR* could also have some articles of interest to you. You do not have to buy all these – visit libraries or use the web regularly to keep up to date with the business press.

Television and radio

It is also important to watch or listen to the news every day, again paying particular attention to business and economic news. Documentaries and programmes about the economy, business ventures, the politics of business and so on can be enormously helpful in showing how what you are studying is applied to actual situations and events. *Panorama* is a good example of the sort of television programme it would be useful to watch. *The Apprentice* and *Dragons' Den* can also be very informative.

Radio 4 offers *Money Box*, while the *Today* programme in the morning has up-to-the-minute reporting on economic and business developments, often with interviews with those most closely involved. It is also a good idea to know the names of the chairman of the Confederation of British Industry (CBI) and the governor of the Bank of England, for example, and the names of the country's top businesspeople. You can make a point of listening to what they have to say when they appear on *Question Time* or *Newsnight* on television, or *Any Questions* on Radio 4.

The internet

A wealth of easily accessible, continually updated and useful information is, of course, available on the internet. Given the ease with which information can be accessed, there is really no excuse for not being able to keep up to date with relevant current issues. Radio programmes can be downloaded as podcasts and listened to at times convenient to you; the BBC's iPlayer gives access to current affairs and documentary programmes for up to a week after they have been broadcast; iTunesU gives free access to thousands of lectures and presentations from universities around the world; newspapers can be read online . . . the list is endless. In this age of information overload, anyone who is serious about keeping abreast of current issues has unlimited opportunities to do so. Thus, an interviewer is not going to be impressed with a student who claims he or she has been too busy to know what is happening in his or her chosen areas of interest.

The following could be particularly useful in your research.

- Subscribe to podcasts and download them regularly. BBC podcasts, which are free, include *Peter Day's World of Business*, *In Our Time*, *Money Box*, *Analysis*, *Start the Week* and *From Our Own Correspondent*.
- Check the BBC news website every day to see what news is breaking.
- If you can't buy a newspaper every day, then look at an online version – for example, www.guardian.co.uk.

> ### Case study
>
> 'My first interview was a disaster. I had written about keeping up to date with current issues by reading *The Economist* and the second question they asked was about that week's edition. In fact, the last one I had read was three months before the interview. After that, they asked me about why I liked their course, and whether it differed in content from others I had applied for. What they really wanted to know was had I read their prospectus. I hadn't, and I got rejected.'
>
> Michael, on his interview for economics

The interview

Interview questions are likely to test your knowledge of business and economics events and developments in the real world. Any relevant controversial topics could well be brought up by interviewers and you should be well informed enough to have an opinion about them from a business point of view.

It is important that your answers are delivered in appropriate language. You will impress interviewers with your fluent use of precise technical terms, so detailed knowledge of the definitions of words and phrases used in business and economics is essential.

You might be asked which part of your A level courses you have enjoyed most. You need to think carefully about this before interview and, if possible, steer the interview in the direction of these topics so you can display your knowledge.

Future plans and possible careers may also be discussed at interview. You will not be expected to have completely made up your mind about this, and, by the same token, you will not be held to what you say at interview after you have left university. Previous work experience is useful and you should be able to recall the precise tasks you carried out during your employment and think about them before interview so that you can answer questions on them fully and well. Questions of this kind will be asked to see whether you have an understanding of how business and management theories and methods are actually applied in the world outside school or college.

Interviewers will ask questions with a view to forming an opinion about the quality of your thought processes and your ability to negotiate. You may be presented with a real or supposed set of circumstances and then be asked to comment on their business implications.

Recent events are very likely to form a large part of the interview and could well be the basis for questions. An ability to see the opposite point of view while maintaining your own will mark you out as a strong business, economics or management degree candidate.

Do not forget that interview skills are greatly improved by practice. Talk through the issues outlined above with your friends and then arrange for a careers officer, teacher or family friend to give you a mock interview.

In any interview situation, it makes a better impression if you arrive in plenty of time for your interview and dress smartly and appropriately (people in business tend to look quite formal).Try to appear confident and enthusiastic in your interview – but listen carefully to the questions you are asked without interrupting, and always answer honestly.

Likely interview questions

Questions may be straightforward and specific, but they can range to the vague and border on the seemingly irrelevant as well. Be prepared for more than the obvious 'Why do you want to study management?' But remember, you wouldn't have been invited for interview unless you were a serious candidate for a place on the course, so be confident, and let your talents shine through.

Many of the following questions could easily apply to both academic and work experience interviews. Try practising your answers to these.

Why have you chosen to study management?

Comment: Focus your answer to this question around how your studies and work experience have provided you with the motivation and interest to pursue this subject at university. This is an obvious starting point for your interviewers and they will probably want you to expand on the reasons for choosing your course that you highlighted in your personal statement. Assume that this question will arise and practise your answer to it: ensure that what you say is well structured and that you do not waffle – try to keep your answer relatively short and certainly no longer than two minutes.

Why do you want to study at this university?

Comment: This is another standard opening question and one that you should certainly be prepared for. You could talk about why the location of the university appealed to you, or how you were attracted to it via a personal recommendation. A prime factor that distinguishes one institution from another is the course it offers. You will need to ensure that you have researched the course in some depth to see what is studied and how it is organised and structured.

Have you visited here before?

Comment: If you have visited the university or attended an open day previously, this is your opportunity to mention it. Remember that the people conducting your interview will have contributed greatly to their department's open day and will welcome your feedback, but do keep it positive! Talk about it being a useful and informative occasion. Your interviewers will expect you to have done a lot of research into your chosen course and institution, so they will be expecting you to be well informed. (The university prospectuses and websites are good sources of information.) You do need to show that you are familiar with the particular institution to which you are applying. Answering this question by just saying 'No, but all universities are pretty much the same' will not improve your chances of getting a place.

What thoughts do you have on what you would like to do after you graduate?

Comment: Of course, you do not need to know exactly what career you would like to follow at the end of your degree at this stage – but you do need to have some thoughts on the kind of job you might be interested in. A possible answer might be: 'I would like a job that incorporates both my education and my practical skills: something combining my A level education with my working knowledge of customer service operations, entrepreneurial abilities and computer and administrative skills.' If, on the other hand, you do have a clear idea about what you would like to go into in the future, then talk about this – but remember to justify your reasons.

How do you think you are doing with your A levels?

Comment: The interviewer will know your predicted grades so you do not need to give too much information about these, but do state that you are working hard and making good progress. Talk about what topics you are studying at the moment and whether you are doing anything related to business and management. Elaborate on the aspects of the course you like, the skills you have gained and/or coursework projects where relevant. This is a relatively boring question, so take the opportunity to direct the conversation towards subjects that you are confident discussing and that will show you in the strongest light. Topics you are happy talking about should be prepared in advance.

What has attracted you to this course in particular?

Comment: This question, like the second one, enables you to show that you have thoroughly researched the particular course for which you are applying. You should draw on a particular aspect of the course that interests you and explain why. The university's website will generally give a precise breakdown of the core units that will be taught each year as well as the optional modules.

Tell me about any work experience you have had

Comment: This is an important question. Expand on the description of work experience that you gave in your personal statement. Do not just list the things you saw and did – mention how you felt about and reacted to what you were seeing and doing. Did you enjoy it? Was there anything that particularly interested or surprised you? Try to give as personal an account as possible.

What are the main things you learned from your work experience?

Comment: This is another standard question that follows naturally from the preceding one. Talk about the varied nature of your experience. There might have been things that surprised you about the functioning of a business or about new technology that was used. How did it differ from your expectations? You could try to link this with things that you have been taught at A level if you have taken business studies, economics or accounting. Work experience includes any part-time or weekend jobs that you might have done. The interviewer will understand that the main reason that you have your Saturday job in a clothes shop is to earn some extra money, but they will be interested in seeing whether you have learned anything from it that might be relevant to your future degree studies. There are many opportunities to do this. Take the example of the clothes shop – you could discuss:

- whether the shop is part of a nationwide chain, or whether it is an independent business – and the advantages and disadvantages of each
- how the shop advertises and markets its range of clothing
- who the target buyers are, and how the business targets them
- how the goods are priced, and who the main competitors are
- the managerial structure of the shop
- the effects of a recession or an economic boom (whichever is relevant at the time of your interview)
- where the clothes are made, and the implications of this for the UK's economy
- customer relations.

How do you keep up to date with current developments in economics?

Comment: Economics (and business and management) issues change every day and to demonstrate a genuine interest in these subjects requires you to keep up to date with current developments. You need to read quality newspapers on a daily basis, watch the news and read specialist websites.

Have you followed any business cases in the news recently?

Comment: As an A level student, you should be reading a broadsheet newspaper every day. Talk about a recent article you have read and why you found it particularly interesting. This is another standard question and it is vital that you prepare your answer in advance. If you try to think of a topic off the top of your head without having given it any serious consideration previously, you could find that you are out of your depth if you have to deal with further questions on the subject.

Have you spoken to any people in business about their work? Have you visited any businesses?

Comment: Talk about people who work in business and what they have told you, and why you have found what they said interesting or motivating. When discussing a business that you have visited, give a different example from the one that you talked about in relation to your work experience. Mention what you learned about the workings of this business and how it operates.

Other possible questions

Below is a selection of questions that have been asked in university interviews. You can use these as a basis for a mock interview. Ask someone who does not know you very well to ask you a selection of relevant questions from the list, and then ask them to assess how convincing your answers are. If there are areas that are obviously in need of work, then you can research in preparation for the real interview. However, do not try to learn 'right' answers to all of these questions and then recite them parrot fashion at the interview. If you do this you will come across as having obviously prepared your answers. There is also a danger that you will try to twist a question to suit one of your prepared answers, and you will appear evasive to the interviewer.

- What areas of business are you interested in?
- How does economics affect your daily life?
- What makes a good businessperson or manager?

- Can you give me a quick summary of the underlying reasons for the credit crunch?
- Why do businesses fail?
- What is meant by 'marketing'?
- Why do share prices fluctuate?
- Is it a good thing that the Bank of England sets interest rates in the UK?
- What is microeconomics?
- What is macroeconomics?
- What is globalisation?
- Is globalisation a good thing?
- Who has responsibility for reducing global warming? Businesses or governments?
- Is the rapid growth of the economies of the BRIC countries a threat to the UK?
- I've got no questions, but you have got five minutes to convince me you should have a place to study here.
- How will the relaxation of the tethering of the Chinese yuan to the US dollar affect this country's economy?
- What will happen if youth unemployment rises as high as 13% in the EU over the next five years as predicted?
- As fuel and commodity prices push up inflation to new highs, how are consumers with lower disposable incomes being affected?
- What is the difference between a U-shaped and a V-shaped recession?
- Tell me about a difficult situation in the past five years that you dealt with badly and explain how you could have handled it better.
- What achievements in the last five years are you most proud of?
- What are your strengths? Give some examples.
- What are your weaknesses? How do you plan to overcome them?
- Why is the course suitable for you?
- I see you have read X recently. Can you summarise the main arguments?

Current issues

Should you be called for interview, the interviewer will probably be looking for a proven interest in and knowledge of current economics issues and/or business case studies. You should already be watching the news and reading relevant publications and newspapers, but you will need to do some extra preparation before you attend an interview. This section is designed to give you an idea of the types of issues that may come up at interview. You will need to do some additional preparation yourself to make sure you are up to date with what has been happening since this guide was published.

The turbulence in the global financial markets in recent years demonstrates the unpredictability of the world of business and finance. Most people would not have guessed that some mortgage companies in the United States that lent money to people with very low incomes would have been the trigger for the collapse of banks and plummeting share prices across the world. Nor would many people have guessed that some EU countries that had experienced significant growth could now be described in the newspapers as being 'bankrupt'. Fluctuating oil prices, based on a range of factors including political unrest and terrorism, have had an enormous impact on people's lives, and the whole oil and gas industries are under scrutiny following the BP oil well disaster in the Gulf of Mexico. Things move very fast in the financial and business worlds: demands change, companies grow and collapse, and political issues affect prices and markets.

By the time you read this, many of the issues that made the headlines at the time of writing will no longer be relevant, and there will be new topics that I could not have predicted making the front pages. Who would have thought, for example, that Facebook shares would drop 49% between the initial public offering (IPO) debut in May 2012 and October 2012? Above all, your knowledge of business, economics and management issues needs to be current. In this chapter, I have included a brief summary of some of the areas that you need to be familiar with. But beware: this is not a comprehensive list, and some of the topics may not be relevant by the time you are applying for your university courses. You must ensure that you prepare properly for your application by reading the quality newspapers on a daily basis, using websites such as www.bbc.co.uk/news to find out what is happening in your particular field of interest, reading magazines such as *The Economist* and watching the news on television.

The credit crunch and the global financial crisis

The credit crunch started with problems in the US housing market. A rise in interest rates caused many people to default on their mortgages, because the mortgage companies had lent them more money than they could afford to pay back. The term 'sub-prime mortgages' describes home loans given to people with very low incomes. The mortgage companies often sold the debts to banks, and so the problem began to escalate. We then began to read about the 'credit crunch' – a shortage of money available for banks to lend to other banks or the public. Some banks collapsed because they ran out of money. When banks collapse, the markets and the public lose confidence because savings are at risk and this has a knock-on effect on share prices. The BBC News website contains a very detailed and clear timeline showing how the problems began, and how they developed and escalated (http://news.bbc.co.uk/1/hi/business/7521250.stm).

Although most countries were emerging from the recession by late 2009/early 2010, it will take many years for stability to return, and many analysts have predicted further problems. Fears were realised when Britain experienced a double-dip recession following two consecutive quarters of negative growth in late 2011/early 2012.

The growth in GDP is a widely used benchmark of a country's financial state, as shown in Table 6.

Table 6 GDP growth for 2011

Country	GDP
US	1.7%
UK	0.7%
Ireland	0.7%

Source: CIA World Factbook, https://www.cia.gov/library/publications/the-world-factbook/index.html

European debt crisis

Following the global financial crisis of 2008, the European Union (EU) has been fighting a crisis that has threatened its single European currency, the euro. During the crisis we have seen governments collapse, a number of countries have experienced a second recession, and political relationships in the region have become fraught as Eurozone leaders attempt to resolve the debt crisis and prevent the collapse of the euro.

Austerity measures saw bailouts being given to struggling countries in exchange for agreed, substantial cuts in spending. Following a bailout for Greece of 110 billion euros by the EU, the International Monetary Fund (IMF) and the European Central Bank (ECB), Eurozone leaders approved a contingency fund of 500 billion euros. Subsequent bailouts have since been given to Ireland, Portugal and Spain. Greece has also received a second bailout as it has been unable to repay its substantial debt.

High unemployment in Greece and anger in the face of austerity measures have led to political discontent, and talk about Greece's possible exit from the euro was widespread. Fear that other countries could follow if Greece left the euro was said by the Spanish government to have undermined its own weak banks, and to have contributed to Spain's need for a bailout.

In June 2012, Greece elected the New Democracy party, which had supported its bailout. The narrow victory was seen as a last chance for Greece to remain in the Eurozone, and fears subsided slightly. Doubts remain as to whether the new government will be able to fulfil the terms of the bailout and repay its debts. If Greece requires loans, and if the rest of Europe is unwilling to help, Greece could be forced to leave the euro. If Greece did default it would set a dangerous precedent and cause investors to become even more nervous, which would be bad news for the Eurozone as a whole.

A country's ability to repay debts is assessed through a credit rating. These are provided by ratings agencies, notably Fitch, Standard & Poor's (S&P), and Moody's. These agencies' ratings determine the interest rates charged on the loans, so a country with a poor credit rating pays more interest than a country with a good rating. The three main ratings agencies assess credit-worthiness in slightly different ways. Fitch and S&P use AAA to denote the highest level, while Moody's rate these countries as Aaa. At the time of writing the USA was at risk of losing its AAA Fitch rating as the country fast approaches its debt ceiling.

The Fitch rating system is:

AAA
AA+
AA
AA–
A+
A
A–
BBB+ etc., down to CCC

Anything below BBB– means that a loan is considered to be highly risky. Table 7 displays the Fitch ratings.

Table 7 Fitch ratings (August 2012)

Country	Rating	Outlook
China	A+	Stable
UK, US	AAA	Negative
Germany	AAA	Stable
Greece	CCC	Negative
Vietnam	B+	Stable

Source: Reproduced with permission from www.guardian.co.uk/news/datablog/2010/apr/30/credit-ratings-country-fitch-moodys-standard.

Oil prices

The supply of oil is controlled by a cartel of oil-producing countries, the Organization of the Petroleum Exporting Countries (OPEC), which decides how many barrels of oil can be sold each month, to ensure that its members get the best possible rewards from their resources. The global price of oil is governed by supply and demand, and by market feelings about the political situation in the OPEC countries (which may increase or restrict supply) and the economic situation in consumer countries (which may increase or reduce demand). Over the last five years oil prices have fluctuated dramatically.

Oil prices more than doubled between January 2007 and January 2008 (following political problems in Nigeria and Pakistan), spiked again in the summer of 2008, and continue to fluctuate dramatically. In 2009–2010, the price of a barrel of Brent Crude rose and fell by over 30%. Conflict in Libya and tensions in Iran have impacted on prices more recently; between October 2011 and March 2012, the price rose more than 25%. Amid worries over the Eurozone debts and an economic slow-down in China resulting in a possible reduction in demand for energy, prices slumped by 30% between March and June 2012.

When the price of oil rises, it affects airlines, businesses, households and the cost of goods. If consumers are spending proportionately more on oil-derived products, their spending on other goods and services will reduce. Because oil is used for transportation in all industries, the over-heads of business will increase. This may either be passed onto the consumer, or, if this isn't possible, companies may have to reduce spending in other ways such as by making staff redundancies. For net importers of oil, price hikes may mean devoting more attention to exports to maintain a healthy balance of trade.

Environmental issues

Rising oil prices, diminishing stocks of fossil fuels and, above all, global warming have changed the ways in which businesses and governments operate. There is a growing awareness among consumers and politi-cians that changes have to be made, and that 'going green' is going to be more than just an altruistic aim. More and more businesses are now trying to market themselves as being friendlier to the environment than their competitors, and governments are keen to show potential voters that they are doing the same. The picture, however, is not a simple one. As an example, take the global rise in food prices. The UN Food and Agriculture Organization reported that global consumption of food has outweighed production in six of the past 11 years, which has driven up commodity prices. Demand for food products remains relatively con-stant but food production can be affected by unpredictable environmen-tal factors such as adverse weather conditions, which can have a significant impact on yield. The 2012 US drought and heat wave in Russia contributed to a 6% rise in food prices in July 2012 followed by a 1.4% rise in September.

One of the industry sectors to emerge from the recession in arguably a stronger position has been green technology, as people have become more aware of the need to promote energy savings and protect the environment. Green technology is described (by the organisation Green

Technology; www.green-technology.org) as encompassing 'a continu-ously evolving group of methods and materials, from techniques for generating energy to non-toxic cleaning products'. Examples that the organisation highlights on its website include the development of alter-native fuels, 'cradle-to-cradle' design (creating reusable or recyclable products), the development of chemical processes that reduce environ-mental hazards, nanotechnology, and 'green building' (the use of local materials).

Microfinance

Another growth area is that of microfinance, providing loans and other financial services to people who would not normally have access to banks or financial institutions. As an example, consider a small village in a rural part of a South-East Asian country. Some people will raise chick-ens, some will keep fish in their ponds, some will grow rice. These peo-ple have very little income, relying on their own produce and bartering – swapping some eggs or a chicken for a bag of rice. The farms are run by the family members, and any extra help is paid with a proportion of the crop rather than a wage. This kind of self-supporting community can work well, until problems arise. If a farmer gets ill, or there is a flood or a drought, the family can no longer take part in the village's informal trading system and so they have to borrow money from private lenders who charge extortionate interest rates, or they have to leave the village to look for poorly paid factory work.

Microfinance – for example, a small loan from a non-governmental organisation (NGO) or a local co-operative – could allow a farmer to buy land, to develop his business, to expand what he produces, buy more stock or employ others, so that if disaster strikes there is an infrastruc-ture in place to allow the farm to continue to support him and his family. Microfinance organisations often set up savings schemes, so that any surplus produce can be turned into money that can be saved and gather interest.

Globalisation

When the UK joined the EU it was known as the Common Market because it broke down barriers for trade between the member coun-tries and imposed some uniformity on trading conditions. Globalisation means that the marketplace has opened up to such an extent that it is very easy to include the entire world. Communication, transport, raising of finance and so on have all become much easier and firms have adapted their business strategies accordingly to improve the way they organise their business. Over half of all international trade is from one part of a multinational to another in a different country.

The standard wage in China has historically been low and firms obviously find it worth their while to build state-of-the-art factories there and ship the goods to their markets in Europe or the US, although the Chinese government's introduction of new labour laws in 2008 saw some multinational companies shift production to neighbouring countries such as Vietnam. Minimum wages are reviewed annually by Chinese provinces, and, as of December 2011, most had raised their minimum wage, with an average growth of 22%. It now varies between £80 and £145 per month, depending on the city. These rises are designed to increase domestic consumerism and may result in more companies moving from China to markets where labour is cheaper.

At first, it was only manufacturing jobs that transferred to the Far East to take advantage of low labour costs; however, more recently, India in particular has become a nucleus for service-industry jobs such as call centres and computer programming. It is obviously impossible for the West to compete against these wage levels and so it has to make the most of those aspects of business where it still has a competitive advantage – in particular, new business ideas.

Businesses in Europe and the US are developing better and ever more efficient ways of managing their brands. 'Think global, act local' is a slogan that is often used in this context to mean that, despite globalisation, different cultures are still more different than we might think. Unless you have a truly international brand such as McDonald's or Coca-Cola, your product might need to be slightly modified for each country.

The West also still has an advantage in technology and innovation, but it is not always easy persuading people to continue paying for this intellectual property. The fact that we can download a lot of open-source software from the internet means that many people no longer pay the licence fee to Microsoft, while MP3s enable people to listen to music without paying royalties to the musicians.

The impact of terrorism

The international threat of terrorism is having an impact on the global economy, but some sectors are feeling the impact more than others. Travel and tour companies have taken the biggest battering to date, due, in the short term, to the psychological impact on consumers who are afraid to fly or visit tourist locations in some parts of the world. Stores that have had major outlets in travel hubs such as airports and train stations have also suffered. WH Smith, for example, saw a fall in share prices and was worried about the effect this would have on trade. Supermarkets, on the other hand, are still trading comfortably, as people are feeling safer closer to home and are not neglecting their regular routines in the light of heightened terror alerts.

Terrorism can have both a direct and an indirect bearing on the economy. It directly affects the economy in the short term with the damage done to people's lives and property, the immediate responses to the emergency and rebuilding of the damaged systems, buildings and infrastructure. These costs, however, tend to be proportional to the scale of the attack sustained. The indirect costs of terrorism mean that investors and consumers lose their confidence in the economy. Strong consumer confidence often goes a long way towards boosting an economy, a particular example being in the US prior to the 2001 terror attacks, and the economy suffers as this confidence wanes. The threat of terrorism can also potentially affect productivity negatively, in the sense that transaction costs may be increased by higher insurance premiums and counter-terrorism regulations. The impact that terrorism has on the global economy is being continually assessed, and its full impact will depend on how long the campaign against terrorism continues and how quickly consumer confidence can be regained.

The growth of China

Businesses have become increasingly international in the last decade and the world has become a smaller place in which to trade. The three regional trading areas – Europe, the Americas and Asia – are all competing for dominance, and the dominant partnerships are ever changing. China has proved that it can live up to its potential to perform on the world economic stage: its economy has experienced an incredible boom since the 1990s and has regularly been showing double-digit percentage growth since then. China became a member of the World Trade Organization in 2001 and is currently working on building the instruments and mechanisms needed to float its currency, the renminbi, on the foreign exchange markets. Businesses in the West have had to make radical changes to their structures, systems and working measures to compete with the lower labour costs and flexible manufacturing systems in Asia, and will need to continue this review to stay competitive in the global marketplace.

The 2008 Beijing Olympic Games also raised the country's profile internationally and allowed China to present its shop window to the rest of the world in an unprecedented way, resulting in increased trade. The 2010 Shanghai Expo offered a further opportunity.

The global economic downturn, although precipitated by the credit problems that affected European and American banks and mortgage lenders, has had an effect on China, however, because the country's growth is based on exports. Nevertheless, China is one of the world's fastest-growing economies; in 2011, it accounted for about one-quarter of world GDP growth. China overtook Japan in 2010 to become the world's second-largest economy (the United States is the largest) with a GDP of approximately $7.3 trillion (in 2011). Average wages are low – China ranks around 100th in the world – but are increasing steadily. Industry is set to overtake agriculture as the biggest employer, while the country's unemployment rate of around 5% is low compared with Western economies.

Costs are also rising in China as the workforce becomes more aware of its earning potential and as the cost of imported raw materials and fuel rises. The minimum wage has risen by 22% between 2010 and 2012. Following the economic downturn these wage increases are designed to increase domestic spending and reduce the country's reliance on exports. This is likely to affect small businesses that are unable to support increased wages, and, combined with a fall in demand for products from the West, could result in closures. There is a shortage of skilled workers, which is driving up wages in bigger cities and means that China stands a good chance of adapting to its slower rate of growth without political unrest.

China's continued growth is also threatened by a shortage of raw materials and energy supplies, and a transport system that is not sufficiently developed to effectively move the enormous amounts of raw materials that the country's industry requires. Social unrest is also a potential problem, as many unskilled migrant workers from rural areas in the west of China, mainly in toy and textile factories, lost their jobs as a result of the global recession and the reduction in the export market and had to return to their home villages. This also resulted in labour shortages in the larger cities in the south and east of the country as the world economy began to recover. China is also, as a result of pressure from the West, spending more money on protecting the environment.

Entrepreneurs

Programmes such as BBC's *Dragons' Den* have raised the profile of the entrepreneur (defined by *The Oxford Dictionary* as 'a person who sets up a business or businesses, taking on financial risks in the hope of profit'). Well-known British entrepreneurs include James Dyson, inventor of the 'bagless' vacuum cleaner, Alan Sugar (Amstrad) and Richard Branson (Virgin).

Although *Dragons' Den* is a very successful entertainment programme, it has highlighted the opportunities and pitfalls of trying to start a small business and, in particular, the steps and capital needed to turn an idea into a profit-making venture. The contestants are quizzed on their marketing plans, the protection of their ideas through copyright, and on how the investors (the titular 'Dragons') would get a return on their investments.

Business case studies

The example below (taken from www.bbc.co.uk) shows how an unexpected or unanticipated event can have a significant impact in the business world. If you are applying to study a business or management subject, you should have some examples at your fingertips of how (and why) companies and businesses grow, decline, change, adapt or develop. So it is vital to keep up to date with such events and the implications of each.

Toyota and car recalls

Toyota sells more cars than any other firm, but, like any other business, has had obstacles to overcome. In 2009, there were safety concerns about a risk that accelerator pedals could get stuck under the floor mat in some vehicles. The company was publically scrutinised for the way it handled the recall of the 12 million vehicles affected and was fined in the US. The Japanese carmaker then struggled to keep up with production demands in the wake of the 2011 tsunami but recovered well, regaining its position as the top-selling car firm.

More recently, concerns over a faulty window switch led to Toyota recalling 7.4 million cars globally. The fault affected 12 models of car and there was speculation that the 'very, very outside chance that there could be melting inside the switch' suggested that there was a fire hazard, damaging the brand's reputation whether or not this was in fact the case. The recall was the biggest of its kind since Ford recalled 8 million vehicles in 1996. Although there had been no accidents, Toyota was quick to act and to defend the company's commitment to quality, suggesting on its website that the recall was a customer satisfaction issue and not a safety concern. Owners of potentially affected cars were contacted and offered a free check of the affected switch, with any faulty ones being replaced.

The announcement for the most recent recall came just a day after a 50% decline in Toyota sales in China was reported. Toyota has been hit badly by the escalating political tension between China and Japan, which has resulted in anti-Japanese sentiment in China. However, despite its recent problems, Toyota does not appear to have suffered unduly: in August 2012, a quarterly profit of 290 billion yen (£2.2 billion) was reported (the highest in four years). It will be interesting to see how Toyota's decision to recall so many vehicles will affect public perception and demand. It would also be interesting to see how the company will compensate for the reduction in demand from the Chinese market.

Other possible case studies

Here are some suggestions for your research (although this is only a very small selection of the many fascinating areas of business that you could look at):

- the successful merger of BA and Iberia, resulting in higher profits thanks to the massive economies of scale and the extension of routes the two airlines can offer
- problems at pharmaceutical giant AstraZeneca as patents on some of their biggest-selling drugs near their end
- Tesco sees profits fall while those at Poundland, Aldi and Primark soar
- the impact of the 2012 Olympics on businesses both in Stratford and around the country
- changes in the airline industry due to oil price changes, affecting both large carriers and budget airlines
- the decline and revival of famous brand names – Marks & Spencer is a good example
- mergers between financial institutions – the global financial crisis has changed the face of banking
- the organic food industry
- how the large sportswear companies have acted in the face of negative publicity about the use of Asian 'sweatshops' that produce their expensive clothes, shoes and sports equipment very cheaply
- Apple's dominance of the music download market and the company's transition from being regarded as a cult brand to being a mainstream company
- the role of social media on shaping businesses (Twitter.com lists a number of case histories of how Twitter has been used by companies such as MTV and Cadbury).

For further examples of business case histories, see the latest edition of *The Times 100 Business Case Studies* online at www.businesscasestudies.co.uk.

7 | Non-standard applications

Not all students who apply for degree courses are studying A levels or their equivalent. The term 'non-standard' could be applied to many different scenarios. Perhaps you are studying for a mixture of examination qualifications, or you have had a gap in your education. You might have already started a degree course in another discipline and want to change direction. Whatever your situation, the first thing you should do is make contact with some universities (either by telephone, or via the email addresses given on the university websites) to explain your situation and ask for advice.

We will look at two of the more common types of non-standard application in more detail: mature students and international students applying from their own countries. These non-standard applicants make up a significant proportion of those wanting to get onto business, economics and management courses.

Mature students

You are considered a mature student if you are 21 years old or older at the start of your undergraduate course. Mature students make up around a third of the UK's student population and in 2011 over 125,000 adults aged 21 or over applied for full-time higher education in the UK.

Mature students fall into three categories:

1. those with appropriate qualifications – for example, A levels – but who did not go to university and are now applying after a gap of a few years
2. those applying for a second degree, having graduated in a different discipline
3. those who have no A levels or equivalent qualifications.

If you are in the first two of these categories, you can apply using the same route as first-time applicants. However, it is worth contacting universities directly to discuss your situation with them and obtain their advice.

A levels need not be the only entry pathway. Many universities now encourage mature students (who could have missed out on the opportunity to enter higher education immediately after school) to apply for entry to degree courses, taking into account their work experience and commitment as part of the entry criteria. There are now Access courses in colleges around the country that specifically prepare mature students for higher education. Mature students make up a growing percentage of the intake of university departments, often coming to their degree studies with valuable relevant experience of the workplace. Your local careers office or library will have details of these. It is also worth contacting universities to see which courses they recognise or recommend.

The main difficulty for mature higher education entrants is that they might not be as accustomed to study as the 18- or 19-year-old entrants. However, they possess an advantage in that they have experienced some of the everyday practical problems they will face in their future careers, and they therefore bring important work skills to their studies. Again, it is worth contacting universities for their advice. As well as being able to advise you on your eligibility for the course, they will be able to give details of the Access courses that they recognise.

Mature students apply using the same application process as school-leavers – UCAS's online Apply system (www.ucas.com) – but whereas a student who is at school or college (or who is taking a gap year) will answer 'yes' to the question 'Are you applying through a school or college?' (and will then be asked for a 'buzzword' – a password that identifies their school or college), mature students will submit the form independently. The main difference is that when the school/college student completes the form, it will be forwarded to the person writing the reference, who will in turn send it to UCAS, whereas the mature student will add the referee details to the form. The referee will then be contacted by UCAS with a login so that they can upload their reference. The choice of a suitable referee depends on the applicant's situation: it could be a current or recent employer, someone who once taught the applicant, or someone who knows the applicant well. If you are in this situation, make sure that your referee reads the information on the UCAS website about how to write a reference, to ensure that it contains the information that the selectors are looking for.

The other main difference will be in the 'Employment' section of the form. This should be as detailed as possible and any gaps – for instance, if you have been travelling – should be explained either in the personal statement or by the referee.

International students

According to UCAS, there were 104,000 international students on full-time undergraduate courses in the UK in 2011–2012. Due to consistent interest from overseas in UK education, almost all institutions will have a dedicated international team able to give advice on applications and accommodation and to support you while you are in the UK. It is well worth making contact with these teams at your chosen universities to find out how they can help you.

International students fall into three categories:

1. those who are following A level (or equivalent) programmes either in the UK or in their home countries
2. those who are studying for local qualifications that are recognised as being equivalent to A levels in their own countries
3. those whose current academic programmes are not equivalent to A levels.

Students in the first category will apply through UCAS in the normal way. All of the information in this book is applicable to them.

Students studying for qualifications that are accepted in place of A levels can also apply through UCAS in the normal way, from their own countries. The UCAS website (www.ucas.com) contains information on the equivalence of non-UK qualifications. Among these are the Irish Leaving Certificate and the European Baccalaureate. Information on the equivalence of other qualifications can be found on the UK government's qualifications website (www.naric.org.uk).

The UCAS website has a section for international students that explains the application process clearly. If you are not familiar with making UCAS applications, I would strongly recommend you visit the UCAS site and familiarise yourself with the process as soon as you can as it can seem complicated. You can contact the UCAS customer service centre or your university choices if you require further help or advice.

Students who do not have UK-recognised qualifications will need to follow a pre-university course before applying for the degree course. These include:

●   university Foundation courses at UK colleges and universities – these normally last one year
●   university Foundation courses set up by, or approved by, UK universities or colleges, but taught in the students' home countries
●   A level courses (normally two years, but in some cases this can be condensed into one year) in schools and colleges in the UK.

A levels allow students to apply to any of the UK universities, including the top-ranked universities such as Oxford, Cambridge and the LSE; however, Foundation courses are not recognised by all UK universities. You should check with your preferred universities about which courses they accept before committing yourself. Representatives of UK universities, schools and colleges regularly visit many countries around the world to promote their institutions and to give advice. You can also contact the British Council to get help with your application (www.britishcouncil.org/about/contact).

UK students applying to study abroad

If you want to spend part of your time at university abroad, you could look at either choosing a course that incorporates a year abroad (usually a four-year course in total), or spending part of your time overseas through the Erasmus scheme. In the Erasmus scheme, you will be able to study part of your degree (three months to one year) at a university in one of the 32 participating European countries. If you want to consider this you will need to check that your chosen university is part of the programme and holds an Erasmus University Charter. All Erasmus students receive financial help with the cost of moving abroad. For further information, see the British Council website (www.britishcouncil.org/erasmus).

If you decide you want to study abroad for the whole of your course, there are some things to consider.

When starting your research, you will need to check that the institutions you are considering are reputable and that the qualification you'll be awarded is likely to be recognised in other countries. You can check this on the UK NARIC website (www.naric.org.uk). Recognition of your degree is even more important if you plan to work in a field where a qualification is an essential requirement (such as law, accounting or medicine). If you're unsure, you can check with the appropriate professional body in the country where you plan to work after you graduate.

There are lots of options for studying overseas in the English language – you don't necessarily have to study in an English-speaking country. It is increasingly common across the EU for courses to be offered in English, and in some cases tuition fees will be lower than those in the UK for EU students. See the Your Europe website (www.europa.eu/youreurope/ citizens) for further information on studying in the EU, fees and entry requirements.

If you plan to travel further afield, you will need to research visa requirements and other practicalities, such as whether this will allow you to work while you study and whether you can apply for any funding, before making a decision (see www.ukcisa.org.uk). See the UK Council for International Student Affairs' website (www.ukcisa.org.uk) for further information and advice on where to start.

Most countries do not have a central admissions service like UCAS, so it is likely you will need to apply to each course or institution individually.

Students with disabilities and special educational needs

If you have a disability or special educational needs, it is a good idea to contact the universities you are considering before you make your final choices. Speak to their student support department and find out how the institution will be able to support you – this might come in the form of extra funding, a note-taker, specialist equipment, etc., and may be an important factor to consider when making your final choices.

An institution cannot discriminate against you based on your disability, so contacting them will not disadvantage your application (under the Equality Act 2010 it is unlawful to treat applications from disabled students less favourably). Institutions have a legal obligation to make 'reasonable adjustments' so that you are not substantially disadvantaged by your condition and are required to do everything they can to foster an environment where all students are treated equally by staff and other students.

The UCAS website has some good information for disabled applicants and recommends asking the following questions (to be tailored depending on the nature of your disability).

- Are all the buildings I need to use physically accessible?
- Are there any particular facilities for disabled students?
- Are there any current students with a similar impairment?
- What support do they receive?
- Who will help organise my support?
- Can you help me apply for additional funding if needed?
- Are the methods of teaching and assessment appropriate to my needs?
- What would happen if I started the course and experienced a problem?

If you are planning to stay in university accommodation and your disability might be important in deciding where you live, make sure you speak to the accommodation or student services department as soon as you can. This will help them to prepare in advance and consider issues such as access arrangements, distance from your faculty buildings and any other special requirements.

Additional funding

Ask your chosen universities about additional funding and do some research into the Disabled Students' Allowance (DSA) as you may be eligible for this.

DSAs are there to financially support disabled students, where a cost is incurred as a direct result of your disability or specific learning difficulty. The amount you qualify for does not depend on your household income, and it does not have to be paid back. Depending on your needs, extra support from the DSA could include specialist equipment, travel costs, Braille paper, a note-taker or a photocopying allowance. More advice about DSAs is on the UK government website (www.gov.uk/disabled-students-allowances-dsas).

Also, make sure you let your funding body know as soon as possible if you think you might need extra help or equipment on your course. The UK funding bodies are:

- Student Finance England: www.studentfinanceengland.co.uk
- Student Finance Wales: www.studentfinancewales.co.uk
- Student Awards Agency for Scotland (SAAS): www.saas.gov.uk
- Student Finance Northern Ireland: www.studentfinanceni.co.uk

8 | Results day

The A level results will arrive at your school on the third Thursday in August. Scottish Higher results come out in early August, and International Baccalaureate results are issued in July. The universities will have received the A level and Scottish Higher results a few days earlier. You must make sure that you are at home on the day the results are published. Don't wait for the school to post the results slip to you – get the staff to tell you the news as soon as possible. If you need to act to secure a place, you might have to do so quickly. This chapter will take you through the steps you should follow – for example, you might need to use the Clearing system because you have not achieved the grades that you needed. Results from other examination systems are not automatically sent to UCAS or to the universities, so you might need to fax or email your results to the universities when you receive them.

A summary of the options available when you receive your results is discussed below.

If you have gained the grades that you need to satisfy your firm choice: congratulations, you have your place! The university will contact you with confirmation of the place.

What to do if things go wrong during the exams

If something happens when you are preparing for or actually taking the exams that prevents you from doing your best, you must notify both the exam board and the universities that have made you offers. It's best if this notification comes from your headteacher, and it should include your UCAS personal ID number. Send it off at once: it is no good waiting for disappointing results and then telling everyone that you were ill at the time but said nothing to anyone. Exam boards can give you special consideration if the appropriate forms are sent to them by the school, along with supporting evidence.

Your extenuating circumstances must be convincing. A 'slight sore throat' won't do! If you really are sufficiently ill to be unable to prepare for the exams or to perform effectively during them, you must consult your GP and obtain a letter describing your condition.

The other main cause of underperformance is distressing events at home. For example, if a member of your immediate family is very seriously ill, you should explain this to your headteacher and ask him or her to write to the exam boards and universities.

What to do if you have no offer: UCAS Extra

If you apply for five courses and either receive no offers or decline all the offers you get, you are eligible for UCAS Extra. Extra operates from the end of February to June and allows you to add one additional choice at a time. You can add an Extra choice in UCAS Track; this will then be referred to the university of your choice for consideration. If this is unsuccessful, you can add another Extra choice as long as it's before June. It's recommended that you call the university to which you want to apply before you add the Extra choice to check whether there is space on the course and to discuss your suitability. If you have not heard back from the university within 21 days, you can add another Extra choice (again, before June).

Students who are not holding any offers when the examination results are published, or who have not been accepted by their choices because they have failed to achieve the grades that they need, are eligible for Clearing (see below).

What to do if you have an offer but miss the grades

If you have gained grades that nearly meet those required for your firm choice (e.g. BBB for an ABB offer) but are good enough for your insurance offer, your firm choice can still accept you if they wish; otherwise, you are automatically accepted onto the insurance place. Check on Track to see whether you have been accepted. If not, contact the university and see whether it can be persuaded to accept you (sample text for an email is given in the box below). Your referee might be able to help with this.

To: r.race@barton.ac.uk
From: Lucy Johnson
Subject: A level results

Dear Mr Race
UCAS no. 08–123456–7

I have just received my A level results, which were:
Mathematics A, Physics A, Economics C.
I also have a B grade in AS Philosophy.

I hold a conditional offer from Barton of ABB and I realise that my grades might not meet that offer. Nevertheless, I am still

---

determined to study economics and I hope you will be able to find a place for me this year.

My headteacher supports my application and is emailing you a reference. Should you wish to contact him, his details are: Mr C. Harrow, tel: 0123 456 7891, fax: 0123 456 7892, email: c.harrow@melchester.sch.uk.

Yours sincerely

Lucy Johnson

If your grades are not close to those required for your firm choice but satisfy your insurance offer, you are automatically accepted on the insurance place. Check on Track to see whether the insurance offer has been confirmed. If there seems to be a delay, contact the university.

If your grades are below those needed for your insurance offer, you are now eligible for Clearing (see below).

If your grades satisfy one of your offers, but you have changed your mind about the course you want to study, you can be considered for Clearing courses if you withdraw from your firm/insurance places. Contact UCAS to withdraw from your original place – you should be careful when doing this as you could end up with nothing if you are unable to find a Clearing place. A sensible thing to do would be to contact your desired university to ask whether they would consider accepting you through Clearing before you withdraw from the course you are holding an offer for.

If you have missing results (for example, an 'X' on your results slip rather than a grade), this probably means that there is an administrative error somewhere, for example a missing coursework mark, or no 'cash-in' code for your AS and A2 exams. Contact your school or college examinations officer immediately to sort out the problem. Contact your firm and insurance choices and explain the situation to them and ask them to hold your place until the problem has been resolved.

Clearing

Clearing is a system that allows students who are not holding any offers to try to get a place on a course with remaining vacancies. You will be eligible for Clearing if you received no offers or rejected all of your offers. If you submit your application after 30 June, you will not be able to make any choices but will go straight into the Clearing system.

If you are eligible for Clearing you will be notified by UCAS and a Clearing number will appear when you log in to UCAS Track. Clearing vacancies will be listed on the UCAS website and will be published in national newspapers following the publication of exam results. If you find a course you might want to apply for, you should first call the university yourself to discuss an application. Have your Clearing number ready and be prepared to answer questions about why you want to study the course. You can add only one Clearing choice so only do this if you have received a verbal offer. When you receive a Clearing offer that you want to accept, log in to UCAS Track and press the 'Add a Clearing choice' button. Clearing places at the top universities are scarce, so you will need to act very quickly.

'I want students in my department who demonstrate that they are genuinely interested in my subject and in my department, and so if I have places left once the A level results are out, I will be happy to consider students who have narrowly missed their offers rather than reject them and give the places to students who are applying through Clearing. Having said that, I have also been able to accept some excellent Clearing students, so I would not discourage Clearing applicants from having a go. But in order to convince me, they will need to act quickly and provide me with evidence – an updated personal statement perhaps, showing reading and work experience, or a reference from their work experience.'

An admissions tutor for business studies

What to do if your grades are better than expected: Adjustment

Adjustment is the process that provides applicants who met and exceeded the conditions of their firm choice the opportunity to reconsider where and what to study. If your conditional firm (CF) choice confirms you, the choice will change to unconditional firm (UF) in Track. When this happens, the option to register for Adjustment will appear in Track. However, you are eligible only if you have **met and exceeded** your original CF offer conditions. It is up to the universities to verify whether you have met these criteria. You cannot adjust your insurance choice. For example, a student who for whatever reason (poor AS grades, illness or lack of self-confidence are all possibilities) applied for courses that required DDD at A level but eventually achieved ABB could then register for Adjustment using the UCAS Track system.

Adjustment is available from A level results day (the third Thursday in August) until 31 August. Your individual Adjustment period starts on A level results day or when your CF choice changes to UF, whichever is later. From this time you will have a maximum of five calendar days (i.e. including weekends) to register and secure an alternative course, without giving up your original firm choice. If you are unable to find something that you prefer, you will still be able to take up your original choice.

Bear in mind that there are unlikely to be places on the most competitive courses available for Adjustment candidates, but it is still worth having a look if you are in this situation.

Retaking your A levels

If you did not get the grades you were hoping for, you may choose to retake your A levels or perhaps just the units that dragged your scores down. If you intend to reapply to university it is worth noting that the grade requirements for retake candidates are often higher than for first-timers. From January 2014 AS and A level units can no longer be retaken in January. Most retake students will need to resit exams in the summer exam session. If you are retaking coursework units you will need to check when this can be done with the relevant exam board.

Independent sixth-form colleges provide specialist advice and teaching for students considering A level retakes. Interviews to discuss this are free and carry no obligation to enrol on a course, so it is worth taking the time to talk to their staff before you embark on A level retakes. Many further education colleges also offer (normally one-year) retake courses, and some schools will allow students to return to resit subjects either as external examination candidates or by repeating a year.

Reapplying

If you plan to reapply through UCAS because you didn't receive offers, decided to withdraw from your application because you had changed your mind about a course or university, or because you did not meet the required grades, you will need to do some research. Some universities will not accept reapplications from students who failed to make the cut the previous year, so before you waste a place on your UCAS form check with the university to which you would like to apply that they are willing to consider a second application. The same can be said if you are applying to different universities but are retaking some or all of your A levels or other qualifications.

If you want to reapply to the same university, contact the admissions department to ask whether they are likely to consider your application. As well as checking whether you will be wasting a choice, it will also give you an opportunity to tell the university in question how much you want to study there. Please see the example email below. Make sure you do not copy it word for word, and that you fully explain your situation and why you may be a more appealing candidate than you were before. If you were required to sit an entrance exam for your first application you will need to contact the university or college to check whether your previous scores can be used for a second application or whether you will need to sit it again.

To: robert.samuel@barton.ac.uk
From: Lucy Johnson
Subject: A level results

Dear Mr Samuel
UCAS no. 08–123456–7

I am writing for advice because I am in the process of completing my application and would very much like to apply to Barton. You may remember that I applied to you last year and was rejected/ was rejected after interview/received an offer of BBB which I unfortunately missed and was subsequently rejected.

I have just received my A level results, which were:
Mathematics B, Government and Politics C, Economics C.
I also have a B grade in AS Religious Studies.

Rather than accept my firm/insurance place at another university/ find an alternative place in Clearing, I have decided to take another year to strengthen my application in the hope that I can be reconsidered for BSc Economics at Barton.

I plan to retake units in both my Government and Politics, and Economics A levels and am confident I can pull these grades up so that I will have BBB overall. I also intend to get some work experience during the following year and have already applied for a number of positions in the banking sector.

What worries me is that I have heard that some universities do not consider retake candidates. I am very keen not to waste a

---

choice on my UCAS form (or your time) by applying to departments that will reject me purely because I am retaking.

I remain very keen to come to Barton and would be extremely grateful for any advice you can give me.

Yours sincerely
Lucy Johnson

If you are retaking and are applying to new universities or courses, you will need to write a similar email to the relevant admissions department explaining what you are doing and asking whether they will consider retake students. Ideally, you would ask your previous school or college to assist you in this.

9| Fees and funding

Studying is expensive. Unfortunately, the reality of being a student is that you are likely to have incurred considerable debt by the time you graduate. This chapter will guide you through how much your course is likely to cost and what funding is available to help you.

Fees

Following recent changes in governmental policy, universities are now allowed to charge UK and EU students up to £9,000 a year for courses (up from £3,375 in 2011). Most universities will charge the full amount, but the amount you pay and the type of funding available will depend on where you are from, which country you'll be studying in and the university you choose.

There is no maximum amount universities are allowed to charge international students; the cost varies and can be found on the individual universities' websites.

Table 8 shows how much tuition fees are likely to cost if you start a course in 2013, based on where you study and where you normally live.

Table 8 Maximum annual tuition fees

Domicile of student	Location of institution			
	England	Scotland	Wales	NI
England	Up to £9k	Up to £9k	Up to £9k	Up to £9k
Scotland	Up to £9k	No fee	Up to £9k	Up to £9k
Wales	Up to £9k	Up to £9k	Up to £9k	Up to £9k
NI	Up to £9k	Up to £9k	Up to £9k	Up to £3,575
EU	Up to £9k	No fee	Up to £9k	Up to £3,575
Other international	Variable	Variable	Variable	Variable

Source: Table taken from www.ucas.ac.uk/parents/studentfinance

Funding: UK and EU students

Tuition fee loans

Wherever you decide to study and whatever your fees, you can take out a loan for which repayments are not compulsory until you are working and earning more than £21,000 per year. The repayment of the loan is calculated as a percentage of your earnings over the £21,000 threshold, so the more you earn, the quicker the loan will be repaid. The tuition fee loan does not depend on household income and will cover the full amount of your fees.

This is slightly different for Welsh students, who have access to a tuition fee loan of up to £3,575. The rest of the fees will be paid in the form of a fee grant which is non-repayable and was introduced by the Welsh Assembly so that Welsh students would not be affected by the increase in fees.

For more information and to check whether you are eligible for the loans, see the student finance section of the UK government website (www.gov.uk/browse/education/student-finance).

Living costs

If you are planning to study full time, it is very unlikely that you will be able to work to support yourself. The amount you will need for rent, travel, bills, books, food and other living costs will depend largely on where you will be living. If you choose to live at home with your parents and go to a local university it will obviously be considerably cheaper than relocating to a major city and supporting yourself.

Maintenance loans are available for UK and some EU students to help with living costs. The amount you qualify for will depend on your household income, whether you will be living with your parents and whether you will be inside or outside London. The maximum amount available is £7,675 per year (for English students from low-income households who will be living alone, in London). See Table 9 (page 94) for more information and for the appropriate website to check whether you are eligible.

This loan will be paid into your bank account in instalments. The amount you owe will be combined with the amount you borrow for your tuition fee loan and you will pay back both together when you start earning over £21,000 per year.

EU students should check the UK government website (www.gov.uk) to see if they qualify for a maintenance loan.

Maintenance grants

Grants do not have to be repaid. If you qualify for a grant you will usually be eligible for a smaller maintenance loan (which does have to be paid back), which means you may receive around the same amount but will owe less when you graduate. The amount you could get will again depend on your household income and your personal circumstances (see Table 9 on page 94).

Additional funding

Some universities offer scholarships or bursaries. These may be offered on the basis of academic excellence, household income, sporting achievement or something else the university decides is relevant. An example of this is the UCL Faculty Undergraduate Scholarship for Excellence (£3,000 per year) offered by University College London, which is awarded for academic excellence. It is a good idea to check directly with the student services department at your chosen university to see if you qualify for any such schemes. Bursaries do not need to be repaid and may come in the form of reduced tuition fees, cheaper accommodation or cash paid directly to you.

Scottish students might qualify for a Young Students' Bursary of up to £1,750 per year, or the Independent Students' Bursary of up to £750 a year. Scottish students studying outside Scotland can apply for tuition fee loans and maintenance loans to cover their costs. You should note that Scottish degrees normally take four years to complete, compared with an average of three years at other UK institutions. Details of support can be found at www.saas.gov.uk/student_support.

There are also grants available from the Welsh Assembly (Assembly Learning Grants – ALGs) of up to £5,161 per year, and a bursary scheme operated by the Welsh universities. Details can be found at www.studentfinancewales.co.uk.

There are a number of publications that give details of funds and bursaries offered by educational trusts, including *The Guide to Educational Grants*, published by the Directory of Social Change. Family Action has a searchable database of over 30 educational trusts, which allows you to narrow down grants based on your own circumstances (www.family-action.org.uk). For scholarship information have a look at the scholarship search website (www.scholarship-search.org. uk). You should also refer to the Educational Grants Advisory Service (www.egas-online.org.uk).

Local Jobcentres also have details of sources of sponsorship from industry and some government departments.

Special considerations

Extra help is available for students with a disability, mental health condition or specific learning difficulty, and for students with children or adult dependants. If this applies to you, you may be eligible for a Special Support Grant or additional support from the university. This may take

Table 9 Financial support available for students starting courses in 2013

	England	Scotland	Wales	NI
Tuition Fee Loan	Up to £9,000 per year	Up to £9,000 per year	Up to £3,575 per year plus a non-repayable fee grant of up to £5,425 per year	Up to £9,000 per year
Maintenance Loan	Up to £7,675 per year	Up to £6,500 per year	Up to £7,902 per year	Up to £6,780 per year
Maintenance Grant	Up to £3,354 per year		Assembly Learning Grants – up to £5,161	Up to £3,475 per year
Bursaries	Ask the Student Support Service at your chosen university about available bursaries and scholarships.		Ask the Student Support Service at your chosen university about available bursaries and scholarships.	Ask the Student Support Service at your chosen university about available bursaries and scholarships.
Additional Funding	National Scholarship Programme for students on low income. University may offer reduced fees, cheaper accommodation or bursary of up to £1,000. Check with each university.	Young Students' Bursary (YSB) of up to £1,750 per year. Independent Students' Bursary of up to £750 a year. Both dependent on income.	Welsh Bursary Scheme – from £347 direct from participating Welsh universities.	Special support grant available for single parents, those with a partner who is also a student and those with certain disabilities.
Further information and where to apply	www.direct.gov.uk	www.saas.gov.uk	www.studentfinance-wales.co.uk	www.studentfinanceni.co.uk

the form of note-takers and scribes for dyslexic students, funds for specialist equipment or additional tutoring. See the appropriate support website (see Table 9) for further information on support grants and contact the student support department of your university to see what support they will provide.

Sponsorship

Some employers offer sponsorship to students on a vocational degree course such as business or management studies. For example, Deloitte runs a Scholars Scheme that includes work placements before starting university and an annual bursary of £1,500.

It is worthwhile enquiring about the availability of any sponsorships by writing directly to companies' personnel departments. You can also get in touch with the university department and the careers service as they may have contacts with particular employers favourably disposed towards sponsoring students. If you are successful, the deal is usually that you will work for the sponsoring organisation during the holidays. This can give you excellent experience and, if you perform well, the prospect of a job offer after you graduate. If you are seeking sponsorship, contact employers as early as possible, as it is common that applications need to be in well before the UCAS deadline.

International students

Fees for international students are not fixed by the UK government, and so they vary from university to university and from course to course. Non-EU students will pay higher fees than UK or EU students. Whereas UK and EU students will pay around £9,000 a year for their degree course tuition, students from outside Europe can pay anything from £7,000 to £22,000 a year for tuition, and it may be even more for clinical science subjects. You should contact your own country's education department, and look at UK universities' websites, for further information. Accommodation and meals will be extra. The cost of living depends on where you study, but, as a rough guide, about £900 a month should cover food, accommodation, books and some entertainment costs. Some governments will sponsor students for their studies in the UK, and some UK universities offer scholarships to students from particular countries, so you should check individual institutions' websites or contact the British Council in your country for more information.

10| Career paths

Graduate unemployment was at a high in 2010 following the recession; although it has dropped since then, it has not yet seen a full recovery. Statistics taken from the Labour Force Survey 2012 (published by the Office for National Statistics) show that graduates still retain an advantage over non-graduates in the jobs market. By October 2011, 86% of all graduates were in work compared with 72% of non-graduates.

Graduates are also likely to earn more. In 2011, the median hourly rate of pay for graduates was 70% higher than for those without a higher education qualification.

Employment prospects vary depending on which degree you graduate with, and the good news is that business-related courses are among those that will lead to higher earnings. The median salary for business graduates in 2011 was 14% higher than for the average graduate; only those with science and technical degrees (medicine, dentistry, maths, engineering, science and architecture) were shown to have more earning power.

High Fliers Research conducted a study of the UK's 100 top employers and found that leading employers are expecting to increase their graduate recruitment by 6.4% in 2012, following a rise of 2.8% in entry-level roles during 2011 and an increase of 12.6% in 2010 (vacancies dropped by 17.8% in 2009 and by 6.7% in 2008). Even though the total number of vacancies is set to increase in 2012, recruiters have confirmed that a third of this year's entry-level positions are expected to be filled by graduates who have already worked for their organisations – through industrial placements, holiday work or internships (see Chapter 2).

Getting into business

Many graduates pursuing a business or financial career have degrees in the subject, but not all fall into this category. Some have studied another subject, such as statistics, psychology or English, and join a company on its graduate management-training programme. Others have completed vocational courses. It is also possible to become a successful businessperson by working your way up through the ranks from the shop floor – but this is much less common today than it was in the past.

Because managers and economists work in so many different businesses and organisations, and their roles vary from organisation to organisation, there is no single route to a career in these fields. However, you will need certain skills and talents, and a strong academic background helps.

Skills and qualities

A degree, even a very good one, is not enough to get onto a prestigious training scheme with a notable company. Graduate recruiters are not usually bothered about your particular degree subject – but they will often want their management trainees to be numerate. Subjects such as marketing, mathematics or statistics, economics, finance or business studies can give you an edge, but some employers still prefer the traditional academic subjects such as history or classics, even for marketing consumer products. However, there are no degree subjects that completely preclude a graduate from entry onto a management-training scheme.

Case study

'The competition to get onto the scheme was intense and we all really had to jump through hoops to secure our places. This started with a fairly straightforward one-to-one interview with the graduate recruitment manager on my university campus. I had prepared well for the interview and had done my research on the company, including looking at its website, and I think this really helped – it certainly gave me confidence. I'd also had a mock interview at my careers service, which was extremely useful. The next stage was an all-day event at the employer's premises. I was with about eight other candidates and we went through a combination of individual interviews with more senior staff and some group exercises, where they gave us a hypothetical problem and asked us to discuss it as a group and come up with some recommendations. I guess it didn't matter too much what our ideas were as long as they made some sense, but I think what they were really looking for was to see how we interacted with each other. That included how we communicated our ideas and also how we listened to others and took their ideas on board. We were also given a 30-minute numeracy test where we were not allowed to use a calculator – so remember to brush up on your tables! I must have passed all those tests, as I was then offered a place on the scheme to start the following September.'

Graham, a graduate in mathematics and management, now a graduate trainee

If you have a good academic background, it will be your personal qualities that will often win you the job. Most companies' recruitment brochures will give you a fairly comprehensive list of skills and qualities they are looking for. Here are some of them:

- communication skills (these are paramount)
- the ability to think logically and clearly and to analyse accurately
- the ability to research facts and to be able to assess what information is important
- absorption: assessment of the importance of lots of very detailed information and seeing its implications
- organisational ability
- the ability to work with anyone at any level and get the best out of them
- building and maintaining working relationships, and summing up people accurately
- the ability to co-operate and contribute to a team
- numeracy
- self-confidence
- sound business awareness
- natural authority and leadership
- the ability to think strategically, see the whole picture and conceptualise
- the ability to keep targets in focus and make sure they are reached
- the ability to motivate others, recognise their potential and delegate responsibility
- high ethical standards
- the ability to prioritise information and tasks.

Career opportunities

Business and management graduates

Graduates in business and management enter a very wide range of careers. These include accountancy, investment banking, insurance, management consultancy, information technology, marketing, business journalism, the media and the legal profession – to name but a few. The list of options is almost endless, but it must be highlighted that many of the careers, and the employers recruiting such graduates, are increasingly global.

How often do you hear someone say 'I'd like to work in business' or 'I'd like to be a manager'? These are not uncommon career aims, but more often than not people do not have a real understanding of what being a businessperson or manager actually involves. The terms are sometimes used as meaning 'being successful' rather than anything to do with the concept of the work. So, first things first: if you are thinking about a career in business or management, you need to find out what management means and what the typical functions or departments in businesses are.

Whenever you open a newspaper and look at the jobs section, every second advertisement has the word 'manager' in its title. Is this just a ploy to attract applicants or is it that some form of management is integral to many jobs? And if so, what do all these people do? Well, they all do different things, and work for an enormous variety of organisations. Yet at the same time they all have certain responsibilities and tasks in common.

The most straightforward definition of management in business terms could be 'the achievement of objectives through other people'. So, the primary difference between managerial and other types of work is that it involves getting other people to do the necessary work rather than doing all the tasks yourself.

Essentially, anyone who manages is responsible – and accountable – for making sure that whatever department or project they are in charge of runs smoothly and successfully. (Depending on the type of employer, this usually means profitably too!) Now this obviously means that you bask in the glory – and, with luck, the profits – when all goes well. But when things go wrong, as they inevitably do at times, the manager is the person who will be taken to task because it is he or she who is ultimately responsible for what happens. So you can draw the following conclusions about the role of management in business.

- Every job has some managerial aspects. Even the most junior clerical workers must ensure that others co-operate with them so that they can do their job.
- No job is exclusively managerial. Everyone has to perform some tasks for themselves.
- Management is not just about status or being paid better. Some professionals and other specialists with no real management responsibilities are often more senior and have a higher salary than many managers.
- The term management also covers a vast range of other activities, including supervision, organisation, administration and leadership. (The job title 'executive' is sometimes used in the same context as 'manager'.)

Management is undoubtedly a skill in its own right and is essentially the same in whatever field it is carried out. Good managers are not confined to managing work that they are capable of doing themselves. Indeed, in the higher levels of management, it can be an advantage not to have the bias that specialist knowledge can bring.

Economics graduates

Many economics graduates follow business or management careers. Economics degrees provide graduates with a range of analytical skills, and an in-depth knowledge of how domestic and global money markets operate. In particular, businesses that operate on a global scale are keen to recruit economists. There are many other opportunities open to economics graduates. Economists are employed by banks and other financial institutions, public bodies, political parties, governments, NGOs and universities. Newspapers often survey the UK's top companies or biggest employers, and the majority of these will employ economists. Some will be banks, accountancy firms or management consultants, but government bodies such as the NHS also recruit economists. The government's own economics service employs over 1,400 economists. Good economists are able to analyse information, mostly in numerical form, and draw conclusions from it. They are generally strong mathematicians as well as being able to understand theoretical models and apply them to real-life situations.

Case study

Jenny studied A levels in economics, mathematics and physics at a sixth-form college in London. She found all three subjects worked well together, and she was able to use ideas and techniques from her physics to help her with her economics.

'I found that being able to understand the ideas behind proving theories and equations in A level physics was very helpful in my economics. In physics, you look at experimental results and then see how they can either prove, disprove or modify an equation or theory. A good example of this is in quantum physics, where one set of experiments seems to prove that light is a wave, whereas another set shows it is a particle – two very different things.

'Economics is the same, but the experiments are on a much larger scale – the global economy, for example! Economists come up with conflicting models to try to explain or predict how economies can develop and change, and we then try to see whether the results of the "experiment" – that is, what is actually happening in the world – support the theories.'

At university, Jenny chose an economics degree course that involved a good deal of mathematical applications, as she enjoyed this aspect of the subject. She now works for a large international bank, looking at the impact of changes in commodity prices and how they affect the economy.

Beginning your career

A number of large companies have graduate training schemes for new graduates. With such companies, training is usually undertaken in-house through formal programmes and on-the-job experience, and is sometimes combined with study for a professional qualification.

However, lots of graduates start their careers in small organisations that may not have any formal training programme. Although this is less structured, it is possible to get a wealth of early experience and responsibility by being thrown in at the deep end, while gaining an excellent overview of how the whole organisation operates.

There is no right or wrong answer when it comes to whether you join a big or small organisation initially. You should consider how much structure and formal training you want and look for an organisation that will give you this. If a firm belongs to the government initiative Investors in People, it will place great emphasis on training and career development. Traditionally, people reach a management position after a number of years of experience in a specialist function, such as sales, marketing, personnel or finance.

Many firms have moved away from the traditional hierarchical structure based on business functions (such as production, marketing, etc.) to one based on project teams. Working in a smaller team like this can be very exciting because there is often a greater sense of urgency and camaraderie among the various members. You need to learn how to reach decisions in a group and realise that everyone is different, but that this does not mean they do not have important skills to contribute. You also learn that no one is perfect and everyone can make mistakes – including you!

Information technology (IT) really has changed the way we are able to work. Some firms now even consist of 'virtual teams', i.e. people who work together but do not share an office. They may be scattered geographically and communicate via their mobile phones and the internet. They may even work for that company on only a few days every week, doing something else for the rest of their time.

Typical business functions

We will now look at some of the most popular areas of business and management in more detail.

Marketing

The marketing function in business is to make people aware that a product or service exists, and encourage people to buy it. This often requires identifying the most likely groups of buyers and targeting them in specific ways. TV advertising, for example, requires considerable planning and market research. Marketing professionals will have researched the product and its rivals and identified how and where they want to place their product in the market to maximise sales, promote brand loyalty or achieve market penetration, and so on. They will commission an advertising agency to come up with a suitable campaign and monitor how this affects sales. Psychologists are often involved in devising advertising slogans or images that will stick in the mind and that will be recalled or influence us when we see the product.

Careers in marketing are often varied; many people who have worked in marketing later move on to advertising agencies or to work as publicity consultants. Marketing tends to attract people who are creative and good at thinking up original and innovative ideas. However, there are also many jobs in market research that require people who can direct discussion groups, design and conduct surveys and process the statistical evidence. For these jobs, it is important to have good numeracy and communication skills.

Most business studies degrees will include modules on marketing. If you are sure that you want a career in marketing, you could decide to choose a joint honours degree such as business studies with marketing, or a single honours degree in marketing. Some art colleges will also offer specialised marketing degree courses, such as fashion marketing. These tend to involve more creative and practical work than those offered on the more traditional courses.

Case study

After graduating with a BA in Business Studies, Caroline started her career as a marketing assistant in the marketing department of a pharmaceutical company.

'The team I worked with analysed markets worldwide to determine which would be most suitable to promote our new products in. This gave me a lot of practical and wide-ranging experience. The company really believes in investing in staff and I was also sent on numerous training courses in all aspects of marketing techniques, so I had a good mixture of formal training and hands-on experience. After a few years, I decided that although I really loved the job in marketing, I'd had a lot of contact with the advertising industry – and that was a big attraction.'

So Caroline decided to try to progress her career in this area: 'I'd built up many valuable contacts through my marketing experiences, so talking to people I knew in the advertising industry helped me identify the sort of jobs I could go for, and the companies that had vacancies. Eventually I was successful – I've just been offered a job as an account executive with a major advertising agency!'

Sales

Another aspect of business is sales. This work is increasingly paid on commission only. In other words, if you do not sell anything you do not get paid. On the other hand, if you are good at selling, the rewards can be fantastic.

What you sell will depend on the business you work in. Books, advertising, professional services, timeshares, cars, stocks and shares, ideas, computer software – anything that a business produces needs to be sold. The work may involve travelling as a rep or may be desk-based telesales, for example. As a manager you will also be responsible for the sales team, whether it is in-house or made up of reps based around the country or abroad.

You can be taught sales techniques as part of a business studies course, but you need a basic aptitude to sell really effectively. If you have natural selling skills, this might be an area to consider. If you are not sure whether a job in sales is for you, your summer holidays could be a useful testing period. There are lots of jobs where you could try out your sales technique, such as working on a stall in a fair or market and encouraging people to come and buy your products, or doing work experience in an estate agents or car showroom to see how the people working there use their sales techniques to encourage customers to make a purchase.

As well as being an integral part of a business-related degree, there are more specialised degree courses available that focus on this area, such as marketing and sales or sales management.

Case study

Neil has been working at a large retail outlet as a department manager for the past two years. He graduated three years ago with a 2.i degree in business studies from Kingston University and successfully got his job by applying through the university milk round. After taking a year off, which combined temporary work with travelling, he joined the company on its 18-month graduate training programme.

'My training has been excellent and I am still learning all the time. I have been on short courses covering topics such as teamwork, negotiating skills, customer service and management skills. I started my training in the soft furnishings department and am now the department manager for the books department. I have been exposed to all aspects of running a department, from working on the shop floor and serving customers to learning about stock-taking and display.

'Each day is totally different – you never know what to expect when dealing with customers. Most are very nice, but you do have to be tactful when dealing with tricky situations. You need plenty of stamina and flexibility, but the rewards are well worth the hard work when you see the sales figures boosted. And the satisfaction of working with your team is tremendous.'

Personnel

Personnel work, or human resources (HR) as it is often called, covers every aspect of a business relating to the people in it. As a personnel officer, you would be involved in the recruitment and training of staff, implementing company policies and government legislation affecting employees and maintaining employee records.

In large companies, HR departments analyse staffing requirements, agree targets and devise selection procedures. They organise staff appraisals and administer training and management development policies, and deal with disciplinary matters as they arise. Personnel departments in some very large organisations will often be split into different functions, such as training and graduate recruitment.

In smaller companies, there might be only one or two people who cover all personnel issues, and these may be a small part of their whole job function. So if you were to join a small administrative department you might get more of an overview of personnel than in quite a large company, where your training might be more specialised. In small companies, it is also quite common for departmental managers to deal with personnel issues such as training and discipline.

Personnel work is often challenging and emotionally demanding. The skills required include objectivity (the ability to see all sides of a problem), a reasonable level of numeracy, organising skills and an understanding of all types of people.

Management degrees are particularly suitable for students who are interested in following this route, because they will include modules on the psychology of dealing with people. There are also legal issues to be taken into consideration – these are also likely to be offered as part of a management-related degree. Most business courses will also provide students with the opportunity to find out more about personnel work and HR, but it is likely to form a smaller part of the course. You might also look at business and personnel or business and HR management courses.

Case study

Alex graduated with a 2.i degree in business studies. In his final year, he took HR management as one of his major options, having decided that he wanted to pursue a career in this area. Despite fierce competition, he was successful in being offered a place on a graduate personnel training scheme with a major accountancy firm, which he has recently started.

Alex is convinced that his one-year industrial placement with a bank helped his credibility. So far, his training has given him a thorough understanding of the firm, and he is now beginning to get involved in some recruitment and selection activities, as well as arranging presentations at various universities. He will shortly be starting the professional qualification for the Chartered Institute of Personnel and Development, which his employer will sponsor. Alex says: 'I know it will be hard work to combine the demands of work with study, but I'm convinced it will be worthwhile and I'm really looking forward to it.'

Finance

The financial aspects of a business are commonly regarded as the most important. If there is no cash in the tills and the bank wants the overdraft repaid yesterday, that spells trouble. All firms have accounts departments responsible for sending out invoices and chasing debtors, paying suppliers and drawing up the company's annual accounts. This is known as financial accounting and refers to keeping track of the financial side of the business after the transactions have happened. Financial accounting lets the senior management know how well the business has done in the past year. However, it does not prepare for the future.

Planning for the future is called management accounting. With this, firms draw up extensive and detailed budgets for every department so that they can keep a tight control on costs and are therefore less likely to make mistakes in the year ahead. Both types of accounting make extensive use of IT.

Accountancy does not have to be boring or deskbound. It can be a good way to join a creative team in the media industry or film industry – areas that are often difficult to get into otherwise.

The financial sector covers a wide range of careers and employers. These include banks, building societies, insurance companies and accountancy firms. All of these organisations would be open to recruiting graduates with a degree in business or management, as long as their A level grades (or equivalent) are good enough and they have a good degree, which usually means a minimum classification of 2.i.

All the major clearing banks run graduate training schemes that give you the opportunity to train and work in many aspects of the bank's function over a period of around 18 months. This will usually mean moving around the country for your various placements. In the case of the banks, you will normally be encouraged to study for the Chartered Banker Institute professional examinations. Once experienced, you might be promoted to, for example, a branch manager. In this role you could be involved with individuals and corporate clients. As a trainee, you might have a spell in a department marketing corporate services and then move into a role as a personal accounts executive.

In addition to their general graduate training schemes, most of the large banks also recruit graduates directly into their computing departments. This does not necessarily require you to have a computer science degree, and most of these training schemes are open to graduates from any discipline. Most careers in the financial sector will require you to be meticulously accurate and good with figures. You will also need to have good interpersonal skills, excellent IT skills and be able to work effectively as part of a team.

Business studies, economics and management degrees will all cover aspects of finance and accounting, as these are equally applicable to the running of a small business, a government organisation, or a country's economy. A business- or management-related degree will look at the more practical aspects of finance – accounting procedures, financial management, legal issues and banking procedures – whereas an economics degree will look at these issues on a larger scale and in a more mathematical and theoretical way.

There are also more specialised degrees available for those students who have a clear idea of their future direction: accounting, accounting and finance, and banking and finance courses are widely available and very popular.

Purchasing

Most organisations, including manufacturing and insurance companies, as well as public-sector organisations, require expert purchasers or buyers.

'Purchasing' is a term mainly used in industry. 'Buying' tends to be used in retailing, and other organisations will often use the term 'supplies'. But the principles of the job are the same. Purchasing managers are now part of a wider profession known as supply chain management. Purchasing is probably at its most complicated in the manufacturing industry, where products such as cars are assembled from many different components. The purchasing manager may be involved from the start, when the design engineers begin to specify the raw materials and the parts needed, by pinpointing suppliers and sorting out any problems with new designs.

Skills required for purchasing include the ability to work well with figures, accuracy, and the ability to digest technical and other data quickly and easily, as well as excellent communication skills.

Business and management degrees will cover topics that are relevant to students interested in this area, and are likely to use case histories and current businesses as illustrations. Economics degrees will include courses in microeconomics (which deals with how individuals and businesses manage and plan their finances) and macroeconomics (how countries' economies depend on income and expenditure). These courses will treat purchasing in a more theoretical and mathematical way. You could also investigate purchasing and supply, or business and purchasing degree courses.

Transport management

Some of the world's biggest businesses are involved in the movement of people and goods, and transport managers are responsible for the safety and efficiency of passenger or freight services. This might include managing and administering places such as airports, railway stations, ports and bus or freight depots on a day-to-day basis. Tasks could include scheduling and timetabling. The role of the transport manager also covers the commercial elements open to all businesses, such as finance, marketing and personnel management.

If there is an accident, it is the job of the transport manager to investigate and take any necessary action. A vital task is to ensure that health and safety regulations are enforced. To be successful in transport management you must be good at organising and planning and enjoy working with figures. It is important that you can remain calm under pressure, but are able to think quickly and logically on your feet. Teamwork and good interpersonal skills are essential.

Both business- and management-related degrees would provide the necessary knowledge and skills for a career in transport management. You could also look at more specialised transport management degrees.

Project management

Many firms organise their staff into specific project teams instead of the traditional functions of marketing, finance, personnel and so on. People on a specific project will come from a variety of different business backgrounds and work together for the duration of that project, often as a team, sharing tasks and responsibilities. You could lead the project as project manager, which requires great skill but can also be very exhilarating.

Management degrees would be the most suitable for a student aiming at project management as a future career. There are many specialised degree courses available, including building project management, project engineering and even public art project management.

Management consultancy

The International Guide to Management Consultancy: Evolution Practice and Structure defines a management consultant as an independent and qualified person who provides a professional service to business, the public and other undertakings. Management consultants identify and investigate problems in a company concerned with strategy, policy, markets, organisation, procedures and methods. Generally, a team is sent to spend time with the organisation to find out what the problems are. It then comes up with a set of recommendations for action by collecting and analysing the facts, still keeping in mind the broader management and business implications.

Finally, it discusses and agrees on the most appropriate courses of action with the client, and may remain at the company for a short period to help implement these strategies.

Management consultants are high-fliers – they can be recruited from the top graduates, but they are usually people with business experience. This is because, if you are going to have any credibility in advising others how to run their businesses, you need real-life understanding of such issues. You will also need to be quite sensitive and tactful and have a good deal of maturity. Excellent numeracy, teamwork and interpersonal skills are all essential, as is a strong academic background (usually meaning at least a 2.i degree from a prestigious university).

Management degrees would provide a good deal of useful background and training for anyone interested in a management consultancy career. Given the need for analytical and numeracy skills, economics graduates would also satisfy this requirement. There are many very specialised management degrees on offer; you can find these using the 'Course Search' facility on the UCAS website.

Case study

Paula joined one of the leading strategy management consulting firms two years ago, following a BSc in Business Administration.

'I chose management consultancy for a number of reasons. The training in business was rigorous and I had to be prepared to work extremely hard. It also gave me the opportunity to meet clients from a huge variety of sectors, which will give me the chance, if I want it later on, to move into industry, having gained wide-ranging experience.

'My first project lasted six months, and I worked closely with three colleagues. I was regularly commuting to the north of England to help analyse and assess why a particular manufacturing company had been consistently dropping profits over a two-year period. After much research, it was the job of our team to feedback findings with a list of recommendations.

'From the beginning I had to get used to presenting my work to colleagues and then to our clients in a clear, logical and persuasive manner. At times, the pressure can be enormous for short periods of time. On average, I work 55 hours per week. I have had two short-term overseas projects, one in France and one in Hong Kong. You are really rewarded for the actual work you do and that is a strong motivating factor for me. I can't think of a job I'd rather do!'

General management in large companies

Large companies will often have general managers who are responsible for the general running and operational details of a business. Their role is to liaise with other departments, monitor how members of staff are recruited and make sure that training is kept up to date. The general manager is also responsible for ensuring that profit targets are met, as well as keeping an eye on the marketing and promotional aims of the organisation.

Several large businesses run training schemes for both school-leavers and graduates as management trainees. Most schemes provide an initial period of training, often 12 to 18 months, in which you are placed in a number of departments in the organisation, such as finance, sales and marketing. This is a great opportunity to try out different areas and find out what you like and what you are good at – a bit like a Foundation course. At the end of the training period, you can decide where you want to specialise.

A number of companies have fast-track management programmes with accelerated training and early responsibility. Many university management departments will have close links with large companies to provide internships or training.

Management in small businesses

Large company management training schemes, especially with blue-chip organisations, are always going to be the most competitive to get onto. You will certainly get a good and thoroughly structured training from them, but you should not overlook the often excellent experience you can gain from a smaller organisation.

In a smaller organisation, you will probably be thrown in at the deep end and are unlikely to have very specific responsibilities, but you will see at close hand the prizes and pitfalls of a career in business. You will also see demonstrated the difference effective marketing can make, and gain first-hand experience of things such as dealing with banks and coping with disgruntled customers – in other words, the reality of working in business.

Managing a small business requires practical skills as well as an understanding of theory. Most business degrees will focus on these skills.

Entrepreneurship

If you have a good idea, have some experience of constructing cash-flow forecasts and are not afraid of failure or hard work, setting up your own company could be your route into the world of business. Richard Branson started his business empire while still at school, as did Alan Sugar. Other useful role models might include the entrepreneur James Dyson or Karren Brady (vice-chairman of West Ham United).

However, it is more common for someone to set up on their own after gaining experience in another organisation. If you are thinking of starting your own business, you will need a lot of the skills and business awareness that are best gained from employment. Added to which, you will need to be innovative and creative, energetic and resilient, persistent and prepared to work long hours. You will need to be realistic in your business plans, and able to adapt rapidly to changing circumstances. It can be very fulfilling to be self-employed, but make sure it is for you before choosing this route.

Successful entrepreneurs tend to be dynamic people with a clear vision of what they want to achieve. Degree courses cannot teach students to be successful entrepreneurs, but a degree in business studies will give a budding entrepreneur the practical skills and knowledge base to supplement his or her ambitions and ideas. There are many degree courses that focus on entrepreneurship, often combined with other disciplines such as mathematics or a language.

What makes a good manager?

Many students are attracted by the thought of a managerial career. It has the advantage of being open to graduates from any discipline and work is rewarded on merit – your worth is judged by your performance. A managerial career does not depend on seniority, and it can offer its own rewards, stemming from practical achievement in a job where results can be measured. While a degree in management will not automatically make you a good manager (just as a business studies degree does not necessarily make you a successful businessperson), it does provide you with the academic and practical skills that are necessary for a successful career in management. Bear in mind, however, that there are other ways to acquire these skills.

Different managerial roles require different skills, but a general idea of what companies require of their managers is given in the next section.

Management skills

Managers today have to work in an ever-changing and complex business environment; they need to use an increasing number of analytical methods and techniques. An important skill lies in knowing which techniques to use in a given situation, and how to use them correctly. Here are the main skills you will need to be an effective manager.

Leadership

Good managers are also leaders. The real challenge of management lies in empowering your team to take charge of a project or goal and together achieve more than they believed they could possibly handle. On a management degree course, you would look at different leadership models.

Delegating

Management involves delegating power and responsibility appropriately, not preventing others from developing by hanging on to everything, but equally not giving colleagues unachievable workloads or putting impossible expectations on them.

Getting things done

Good managers are the people who get things done, and they do this by inspiring and encouraging the people working with them.

Teamwork

Teamwork plays a huge part in successful management and is the main reason why employers frequently ask candidates about their extracurricular achievements and activities. Playing a sport, taking part in dramatic productions or being involved in a school magazine or university society all show an ability to work in a team.

Managing your own work

It is essential that the good manager is effective at managing their own workload well and setting standards for their team. This means setting an example in areas such as good organisation, timekeeping, commitment, personal presentation and honesty.

Managing stress

Because of the pressures of management, good managers will do whatever they can to avoid the effects of undue stress on their physical and mental health – and therefore their productivity. This means having problem-solving skills: you will need to notice if a stressful situation is developing and affecting a team or its members, and be able to deal with it successfully.

Political awareness

Every organisation has its own culture and politics. Good managers will be aware of the context in which they work, including the sensitivities of other people and other departments, so that they can be most effective at motivating their teams.

Managing functions

The management role is broad ranging, and responsibilities can be spread over several business areas or functions. For example:

- operations: maintaining and improving delivery of the service or product for which they are responsible
- finance: budgeting and monitoring the use of resources
- people: motivating those they work with
- information: communicating effectively with everyone at all levels.

Languages

Language skills are essential, and already more than half of the world's population speak a second language. To enable effective communication with others, you need to cope with the nuances of speech as well as understanding documents such as letters and reports. If you are an English speaker you can get by in Scandinavia, the Netherlands, Germany, much of Central and Eastern Europe and sometimes in France and Belgium without local language skills. (This would not, perhaps, be so easy in Spain or Italy.) But in any situation, you will always be at an advantage if you are able to hold at least a simple conversation in the language of the country in which you are working.

11 | Further information

The UCAS tariff

Full details of the UCAS tariff point system can be found on the UCAS website. For A levels and AS levels, the tariff point system is shown in Table 10.

So, a university might ask for 300 points, and the offer might specify that this applies to three A level subjects. To satisfy the offer, the student would need to achieve at least ABC, AAD or BBB. If the offer allows the student to include the fourth AS subject, some of the combinations totalling 360 points that would be acceptable are shown in Table 11.

If you receive a 'points' offer from a university, you should ensure that you are clear whether it includes just the A level grades, the A level and AS grades, or whether other qualifications that have a UCAS tariff (such as Key Skills or certain music examinations) can be included as well.

Tables 10–14 are reprinted with kind permission of UCAS.

Other qualifications and the tariff point system

Tariff points offered for the International Baccalaureate, the Irish Leaving Certificate and the Scottish Highers are shown in Tables 12–14.

Table 10 The UCAS tariff point system

AS level grade	UCAS tariff points	A level grade	UCAS tariff points
A	60	A*	140
B	50	A	120
C	40	B	100
D	30	C	80
E	20	D	60
		E	40

Table 11 Combinations of grades that total 360 points

A level	AS level
AAB	E
ABB	C
BBB	A

Table 12 International Baccalaureate tariff points

B grade	Tariff points
45	720
44	698
43	676
42	654
41	632
40	611
39	589
38	567
37	545
36	523
35	501
34	479
33	457
32	435
31	413
30	392
29	370
28	348
27	326
26	304
25	282
24	260

Table 13 Irish Leaving Certificate tariff points

Grade: Higher	Grade: Ordinary	Tariff points
A1		90
A2		77
B1		71
B2		64
B3		58
C1		52
C2		45
C3	A1	39
D1		33
D2	A2	26
D3	B1	20
	B2	14
	B3	7

Table 14 Scottish Highers tariff points

| Advanced Higher | | Higher | | Scottish Interdisciplinary Project | | Scottish National Certificate* | |
Grade	Tariff points	Grade	Tariff points	Grade	Tariff points	Grade	Tariff points
A	130	A	80	A	65	Group C	125
B	110	B	65	B	55	Group B	100
C	90	C	50	C	45	Group A	75
D	72	D	36				

*Points for Scottish National Certificates came into effect for entry into higher education from 2011 onwards.

Subjects covered by each Scottish National Certificate group (see table 14)

Group A	Group B	Group C
Advertising and Public Relations	Acting and Theatre Performance	Beauty Care
Applied Sciences	Aeronautical Engineering	Electronic Engineering
Art and Design	Computer Arts and Animation	Fabrication and Welding Engineering
Building Services Engineering	Computing: Technical Support	Hairdressing
Built Environment	Early Education and Childcare	Make-Up Artistry
Civil Engineering	Electrical Engineering	Manufacturing Engineering
Computer Aided Design with Technology	Engineering Systems	Measurement and Control Engineering
Creative Printmaking with Photography	Fashion Design and Manufacture	Mechanical Engineering
Digital Media	Health and Social Care	Technical Theatre
Computing Media	Land-based Engineering	Wellness Therapies
Model Making: TV and Film	Pharmacy Services	
Music	Professional Cookery	
Sound Production	Shipping and Maritime Operations	
Travel and Tourism	Working with Communities	

Useful addresses

Association of Chartered Certified Accountants (ACCA)
29 Lincoln's Inn Fields
London WC2A 3EE
Tel: 020 7059 5000
Web: www.acca.org.uk

British Chambers of Commerce
65 Petty France
London SW1H 9EU
Tel: 020 7654 5800
Web: www.britishchambers.org.uk

Chartered Institute of Logistics and Transport
Earlstrees Court
Earlstrees Road
Corby NN17 4AX
Tel: 01536 740100
Web: www.ciltuk.org.uk

Chartered Institute of Management Accountants
26 Chapter Street
London SW1P 4NP
Tel: 020 8849 2251
Web: www.cimaglobal.com

Chartered Institute of Marketing
Moor Hall
Cookham
Maidenhead SL6 9QH
Tel: 01628 427120
Web: www.cim.co.uk

Chartered Institute of Personnel and Development
151 The Broadway
London SW19 1JQ
Tel: 020 8612 6200
Web: www.cipd.co.uk

Chartered Institute of Purchasing and Supply
Easton House
Church Street
Easton on the Hill
Stamford PE9 3NZ
Tel: 01780 756777
Web: www.cips.org

Chartered Management Institute
Management House
Cottingham Road
Corby NN17 1TT
Tel: 01536 204222
Web: www.managers.org.uk

Chartered Quality Institute
2nd Floor North
Chancery Exchange
10 Furnival Street
London EC4A 1AB
Tel: 020 7245 6722
Web: www.thecqi.org

Confederation of British Industry (CBI)
Centre Point
103 New Oxford Street
London WC1A 1DU
Tel: 020 7379 7400
Web: www.cbi.org.uk

Department for Employment and Learning of Northern Ireland
Adelaide House
39–49 Adelaide Street
Belfast BT2 8FD
Tel: 028 9025 7777
Web: www.delni.gov.uk

Federation of Small Businesses
Sir Frank Whittle Way
Blackpool FY4 2FE
Tel: 0808 20 20 888
Web: www.fsb.org.uk

Freight Transport Association
Hermes House
St John's Road
Tunbridge Wells TN4 9UZ
Tel: 01892 526171
Web: www.fta.co.uk

Higher Education Funding Council for England
External Relations Department
Northavon House
Coldharbour Lane
Bristol BS16 1QD
Tel: 0117 931 7317
Web: www.hefce.ac.uk

Higher Education Funding Council for Wales
Linden Court
Ilex Close
Llanishen
Cardiff CF14 5DZ
Tel: 029 2076 1861
Web: www.hefcw.ac.uk

Institute of Administrative Management
6 Graphite Square
Vauxhall Walk
London SE11 5EE
Tel: 020 7091 2600
Web: www.instam.org

Institute of Chartered Secretaries and Administrators
16 Park Crescent
London W1B 1AH
Tel: 020 7580 4741
Web: www.icsaglobal.com

Institute of Credit Management
The Water Mill
Station Road
South Luffenham LE15 8NB
Tel: 01780 722900
Web: www.icm.org.uk

Institute of Directors
116 Pall Mall
London SW1Y 5ED
Tel: 020 7766 8866
Web: www.iod.com

Institute of Management Services
Brooke House
24 Dam Street
Lichfield WS13 6AA
Tel: 01543 266909
Web: www.ims-productivity.com

Institute of Materials, Minerals and Mining
1 Carlton House Terrace
London SW1Y 5DB
Tel: 020 7451 7300
Web: www.iom3.org

Management Consultancies Association
60 Trafalgar Square
London WC2N 5DS
Tel: 020 7321 3990
Web: www.mca.org.uk

Operational Research Society
Seymour House
12 Edward Street
Birmingham B1 2RX
Tel: 0121 233 9300
Web: www.theorsociety.com

Prince's Trust
18 Park Square East
London NW1 4LH
Tel: 020 7543 1234
Web: www.princes-trust.org.uk

Scottish Funding Council
Donaldson House
97 Haymarket Terrace
Edinburgh EH12 5HD
Tel: 0131 313 6500
Web: www.sfc.ac.uk

Work Foundation
21 Palmer Street
London SW1H 0AD
Web: www.theworkfoundation.com

Books

General higher education

Choosing Your Degree Course & University, 13th edition, Brian Heap, Trotman

Getting into Oxford and Cambridge: 2014 entry, 16th edition, Jenny Blaiklock, Trotman

Cut the Cost of Uni: How to Graduate with Less Debt, Gwenda Thomas, Trotman

HEAP 2014: University Degree Course Offers, 44th edition, Brian Heap, Trotman

How to Complete Your UCAS Application: 2014 entry, 25th edition, Beryl Dixon, Trotman

Business, economics and management

Bounce: The Myth of Talent and the Power of Practice, Matthew Syed, HarperCollins

Business Stripped Bare: Adventures of a Global Entrepreneur, Sir Richard Branson, Virgin Books

Business: The Ultimate Resource, Chris Bartlett, Meredith Belbin and Warren Bennis, A & C Black

Cityboy: Beer and Loathing in the Square Mile, Geraint Anderson, Headline

The Credit Crunch: Housing Bubbles, Globalisation and the Worldwide Economic Crisis, Graham Turner, Pluto Press

Economics for Business and Management, Alan Griffiths and Stuart Wall, Pearson Education

Effective Small Business Management, Norman M. Scarborough, Pearson Education

The Essential Drucker: The Best of Sixty Years of Peter Drucker's Essential Writings on Management, Peter Drucker, HarperCollins

Essential Manager's Manual, Robert Heller and Tim Hindle, Dorling Kindersley

Freakonomics: A Rogue Economist Explores the Hidden Side of Everything, Steven D. Levitt and Stephen J. Dubner, Penguin

How I Caused the Credit Crunch, Tetsuya Ishikawa, Icon Books

How Markets Fail: The Logic of Economic Calamities, John Cassidy, Penguin

Human Resource Management: A Contemporary Approach, Julie Beardwell and Tim Claydon, Pearson Education

Iconoclast: A Neuroscientist Reveals How to Think Differently, Gregory Berns, Harvard Business School Press

Innovation and Entrepreneurship, Peter F. Drucker, Butterworth Heinemann

The New Pioneers: Sustainable Business Success Through Social Innovation and Social Entrepreneurship, Tania Ellis, John Wiley & Sons

No Logo, Naomi Klein, Fourth Estate

The Real Deal: My Story from Brick Lane to Dragons' Den, James Caan, Virgin Books

Reinventing Management: Smarter Choices for Getting Work Done, Julian Birkinshaw, John Wiley & Sons

The Shock Doctrine: The Rise of Disaster Capitalism, Naomi Klein, Penguin

The Snowball: Warren Buffett and the Business of Life, Alice Schroeder, Bloomsbury

Superfreakonomics: Global Cooling, Patriotic Prostitutes and Why Suicide Bombers Should Buy Life Insurance, Steven D. Levitt and Stephen J. Dubner, Penguin

The Undercover Economist, Tim Harford, Abacus

What They Teach You at Harvard Business School: My Two Years Inside the Cauldron of Capitalism, Philip Delves Broughton, Penguin

Whoops!: Why Everyone Owes Everyone and No One Can Pay, John Lanchester, Penguin

Useful websites

Business and financial news

www.bbc.co.uk/news
www.businessweek.com
www.economist.com
www.ft.com
www.telegraph.co.uk/finance

Financial organisations

www.wto.org
www.worldbank.org

University entrance

www.ucas.com
www.guardian.co.uk/education/universityguide

Glossary

Adjustment

A UCAS process allowing students who met and exceeded conditions of their firm choice to be considered by alternative courses, without having to let go of their firm choice.

Administration

A process which allows struggling companies to attempt a comeback by allowing them to continue to operate under close supervision. Companies in Administration need permission from a court before they can be dissolved.

Austerity

A policy implemented by government to reduce deficit. This will involve spending cuts which often means a reduction in benefits and public services. It may also mean increases in taxation.

Bailout

The provision of financial assistance to a government or business in order to prevent the consequences that would arise from its financial collapse. This may be provided in the form of a loan, stocks, cash, bonds or guaranteeing of assets/debts. A bailout may come with terms attached and may or may not have to be repaid.

Balance of trade

The difference in countries' earnings from export and the amount it spends on imports.

BRIC

Brazil, Russia, India and China. Sometimes referred to as the 'Big Four', the economies of these developing countries are growing very fast.

Clearing

A UCAS system that allows students who are not holding any offers to try to get a place on a course with remaining vacancies.

Common market

A group of countries that have agreed to promote duty-free trade and free movement of labour between members. They also agree to set common tariffs for imports coming from outside member countries. The European community is a good example of this.

Confederation of British Industry (CBI)
A lobbying organisation that looks after the interests of British businesses at home and overseas. By working with government bodies and legislators it seeks to promote conditions in which British business can compete and thrive.

Credit crunch
A condition where borrowing is difficult because of fears about the ability of borrowers to repay loans. A shrinking credit supply will slow economic growth and it becomes more difficult for borrowers to repay existing debts.

Default
The failure to meet the terms of a loan or another debt.

Deficit
A shortfall in revenue. A government budget deficit describes a situation where the amount a government spends is greater than its income.

Deflation
Negative inflation, where the prices of commodities and services drop on average across the economy.

Double-dip recession
A secondary recession following a brief recovery from a previous period of negative growth.

ECB
The European Central Bank, responsible for monetary policy in the Eurozone. Specifically it aims to keep inflation low and prevent deflation.

Eurozone
An economic and monetary union of the 17 countries which use the Euro as their common currency.

Extra
A UCAS process that allows you to add one extra choice at a time (between February and June) if you are holding no offers.

GDP
Gross domestic product. The market value of goods and services produced within a country during a one year period (plus the value of exports minus the value of imports). It is an indicator of economic activity for a country during a specified period.

IMF
The International Monetary Fund. An organisation set up after World War II to provide financial assistance to governments. The IMF has provided rescue loans to developing countries with debt issues, and more recently has been involved in bailouts for EU governments during the European debt crisis.

Inflation
An increase in prices of goods and services in an economy over a period of time.

Macroeconomics
The study of economic issues across a whole economy. It looks at economy-wide patterns in areas such as trade.

Microeconomics
The study of choices made by individuals and businesses in order to better understand behaviour. Microeconomists often use this sort of information to understand supply and demand in particular markets (e.g. oil or coffee) and to make predictions about how markets will react to external influences.

OPEC
The Organization of the Petroleum Exporting Countries. It currently consists of 12 countries: Algeria, Angola, Ecuador, Iran, Iraq, Kuwait, Libya, Nigeria, Qatar, Saudi Arabia, the United Arab Emirates and Venezuela.

Personal statement
This is where you have 47 lines (or 4,000 characters including spaces, whichever you use first) to convince the five universities you are applying to that you are right for the course.

Recession
A slowdown in economic activity. A country is technically in recession following two consecutive periods of negative growth.

UCAS
Universities and Colleges Admissions Service.